a guy's guide to growing up

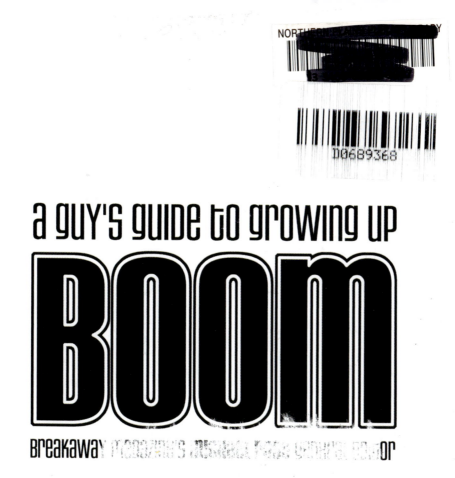

BOOM

Breakaway _____or

a guy's guide to growing up

BOOM

Breakaway magazine's **michael ross** general editor

TYNDALE

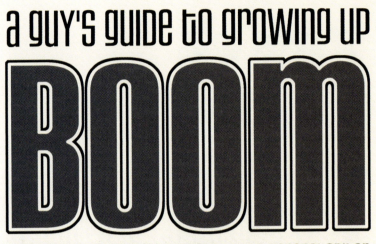

a guy's guide to growing up
BOOM
Breakaway magazine's michael ross general editor

©2003 by Focus on the Family. All rights reserved. International copyright secured.

Library of Congress Cataloging-in-Publication Data
Boom : a guy's guide to growing up / Michael Ross, general editor.
p. cm.
Includes bibliographical references.
ISBN 1-58997-060-8
1. Teenage boys—Religious life. 2. Christian life. I. Ross, Michael, 1961-
BV4541.3.B66 2003
248.8'32—dc21
2003008693

A Focus on the Family Book published by Tyndale House Publishers, Wheaton, Illinois.

Unless otherwise noted, Scripture quotations are from the HOLY BIBLE, NEW INTERNATIONAL VERSION®.
©1973, 1978, 1984 by the International Bible Society.
Used by permission of Zondervan Publishing House. All rights reserved.

The use of material from various Web sites does not imply endorsement of those sites in their entirety.

Portions of chapter 19 were written by Steven Isaac, the associate editor of Focus on the Family's *Plugged In*.

Focus on the Family books are available at special quantity discounts when purchased in bulk by
corporations, organizations, churches, or groups.
Special imprints, messages, and excerpts can be produced to meet your needs. For more information, contact:
Resource Sales Group, Focus on the Family,
8605 Explorer Drive, Colorado Springs, CO 80920; phone (800) 932-9123.

Editor: Ray Seldomridge
Design: Lance Blanchard

Printed in the Singapore

02 03 04/10 9 8 7 6 5 4 3 2 1

meet the guys WHO WROTE THIS BOOK ▌▌▌ ▌▌ ▌

michael ross is the editor of *Breakaway,* a national magazine for teen guys published by Focus on the Family. Communicating with teenagers is his passion. Aside from being a writer and the general editor for this guide, Michael has written a bunch of other books for young people. He also loves adventure travel. His most memorable trip was a safari through Zimbabwe by motorcycle (with a bunch of teens, of course), then by boat down the Zambezi River.

Jeremy V. Jones is the associate editor of *Breakaway.* His job takes him all over the country, landing interviews with athletes, musicians, and cool, everyday teens just like you. Highlights include learning to shred for a surfing story and hanging out with some firefighters for a write-up on these brave men and women.

chuck johnson is the director of periodicals at Focus on the Family. In other words, he spends his time leading and motivating people. (Hey, he used to be a high school principal, so he has lots of experience!)

bob smithouser is an entertainment expert and the editor of *Plugged In,* a media magazine published by Focus on the Family. Bob also writes "High Voltage," a popular column in Breakaway.

manfred koehler is a Canadian-born missionary to Mexico as well as a frequent contributor to Breakaway. Manfred's number-one mission is helping young people know and serve Jesus Christ.

jeff edmondson is a cool youth guy (he speaks to teens all over the world), a contributor to *Breakaway,* and a card-carrying sci-fi fan. He's practically a walking *Star Trek* encyclopedia!

contents ▐▐▐ ▐▐ ▐ ▐ ▐▐▐▐ ▐▐ ▐

INTRODUCTION

- Why am I so girl-crazy?
- What's happening to my body?
- How can I make friends?
- I get picked on a lot—what should I do?
- Will I ever grow taller, like the other guys?
- Why do my parents drive me nuts?
- How can I get a clue about God's will for my life?
- I think about sex all the time—is this normal?
- HELP! Everything feels sorta weird right now.

I need advice about all kinds of private guy stuff—
BUT WHERE CAN I GO FOR ANSWERS?!

Questions. Tons of them are swirling around that brain of yours. And who can blame you if you're feeling a little freaked out—maybe even BIG-TIME freaked out? After all, your world is totally changing.

It's as if you're in the cockpit of an F-16 fighter that's blasting through the clouds at Mach 2. The once-safe place you knew as a boy is long behind you now. Just ahead: a vast, hostile, foreign land known as "Manhood." Will you measure up in this strange new world? Will you survive? Will you find your mission, especially the one God has for you?

Don't panic! Instead, take a deep breath and chill out, because we have some awesome news: Your hot little hands are grasping your very own mission manual. That's right! Think of this book as a user's guide to being a teen guy. We've filled these pages with all kinds of answers to just about everything you need to know—even about the most secret, most scary, most embarrassing . . . MOST PRIVATE guy issues.

As you make your way through this guide, you'll find lots of tips on how to relate, communicate, and interact with those cool creatures known as girls.

You'll find plenty of advice on lots of other stuff as well: dating, purity, God's design for sex, courtship, crushes, kissing, lust control, friendships, popularity, bullying, body changes, masturbation, zit attacks, emotions, working out, boosting your confidence, connecting with parents, relating to teachers, building a stronger faith, setting goals, selecting music, watching movies, navigating the Internet, playing computer games . . . and a bunch of tips about money (making it, spending it, saving it).

Oh, and did we mention advice about girls?

Cool!

part one: Becoming a man

CHAPTER ONE: get a LIFE!

You're becoming a man, but do you have a life yet?

We're not talking about physical life. If you're reading this, you've already got that. We're talking about a life of meaning, joy, and peace, a life with no regrets. We're talking about the life God designed you to live.

Need some clues on how to get this kind of life? Keep reading!

ULTIMATE MAN—ULTIMATE LIFE!

Brian Decker, running back, couldn't keep his mind on football practice. Words from this summer's Bar J Youth Camp kept twirling through his mind—Jesus' words, no less: *"I am the way, the truth and the life."*

From what seemed like miles away, Brian heard the numbers called, the ball hiked, the bodies clash. Vaguely, he remembered something. A 10-yard buttonhook. Running as if through fog, he hardly felt the coming shoulder pad. Knocked off balance, he fought to stay on his feet. No such luck. As his helmet ground its way into the 42-yard hash mark, the words kept coming: *"No one comes to the Father except through me."*

Rolling over, Brian stared into the oncoming face of an angry Phil Bellos, the team captain. Crouching on one knee, Bellos let his mouth guard drop. It dripped in Brian's face. The captain cracked a nasty smile. The mouth guard dripped again. With Bellos's spit dribbling down his cheek, Brian was back at the Bar J. *"I am . . ."*

Bellos frowned. "You brainless toad. You haven't made a single play all afternoon. Isn't it about time you get a life?"

Those last words hit like a 400-pound lineman.

Brian was on his feet so fast that Bellos jerked two steps back, eyes wide. Brian was half Bellos's size, but he didn't care. With one step, he was in Bellos's face, their helmets tapping. Slowly, Brian let his own mouth guard slip from his lips.

The words still pounded inside his head: *"I am the way, the truth and the . . ."*

" 'Get a life'?" he said. "Best advice I've heard in a long time!"

WHERE DOES THAT KIND OF LIFE COME FROM?

Extreme sports offer "life on the edge." Beer commercials promise "real living." Drug dealers push "a life of ecstasy." The Marlboro man sells "cool living." At best, these things can distract us from true life. At worst, they're death in disguise.

Jesus Christ, the ultimate Man, is the only one who can deliver on His promise of life to the ultimate (John 10:10). He's already gone a long way to bring it to you. He's the Man who bravely faced an unjust death sentence without a word. He shed His blood. He defeated death. His life can be your life, if only you'll believe and receive (John 1:12).

BUT WHEN AND WHERE DOES THAT LIFE START?

Christ's life does not start somewhere in the vague future (after death) or in some distant location (way off in heaven). Christ's life starts the moment you trust Him. Moreover, Christ's life makes its home in your heart, your soul, your very being.

If you're a believer, Christ's life is now. If you're one of His followers, Christ's life is where you stand.

IS THE LIFE OF CHRIST WORTH LIVING?

That is the ongoing question of a lifetime. Some people conclude, quite simply, no. Christ's life—at least their understanding of it—is a drag. But they're wrong. Flat out.

To view Christ's life as boring is to be badly misinformed. Such people haven't discovered the truth. Anyone suffering with "drag syndrome" hasn't got a life yet. The truth is, Christ's life is packed with challenges, risks, rewards, giants, victories, mountains, miracles, and sheer heart-gripping excitement.

Walking with Jesus, living His life, is a whole new adventurous assignment every day.

Be a real man—plunge into adventure. Christ, in giving you His life, enables you to run a race (Hebrews 12:1), discover great riches (Romans 11:33), go into battle (2 Timothy 2:3-4), wrestle with demons (Ephesians 6:12), and even hold your ground against Satan himself (Ephesians 6:10-11). God's plan for you, lived in the strength of Christ's life, is the odyssey of a lifetime—yours for the taking.

Get a real life—follow Christ. Most of the world doesn't know what this means. But you do, if you're convinced of this: *Christ's life is the only life worth living.* Make that thought a banner in your soul.

Take the challenge—start the adventure. Once you're convinced, you're ready for the nitty-gritty details on what living Christ's life looks like.

are you "cross-eyed"?

Living Christ's life involves diving deep into Jesus' words in Matthew 16:24: "If anyone would come after me, he must deny himself and take up his cross and follow me."

- Deny myself? What's that mean?
- Take up my cross? You mean, like, get crucified?
- Follow Jesus? He isn't even around!

Valid questions. If you're asking them, great. Most people read that verse, nod their heads at the holy-sounding words, and read on. But you're different. You want the real-life implications of what Jesus is saying. Let's take this a piece at a time.

deny myself? what does this really mean?

Too many people wake up each morning thinking, *What do I want to do today?* Their concern is with where *I* want to go, what *I* want to say, what *I* want to accomplish. Mankind's natural tendency is to always think in terms of me, myself, and I.

In contrast, "denying myself" pushes that natural tendency aside. It's saying no to me and yes to God. Christ's life is not about me; it's about Jesus. If I am to enjoy Christ's life, the main question can no longer be "What do I want to do?" The big question now becomes "What does Christ want me to do?"

That big question is something you need to ask yourself a dozen times—or better yet, a hundred times—a day: "Jesus, what's next?" Whenever you are more concerned with what your Savior wants than with what you want, you are "denying yourself."

Try it. Ask yourself the question right now: "Jesus, what do You want me to do with the next few minutes of my life?" Go ahead. Ask Him.

Most likely, He'll suggest you keep reading. If you obey Him and keep reading (rather than picking up the Game Boy you just saw), you've "denied yourself." Way to go.

Now make it a habit. The more of a habit it becomes, the more you'll experience Christ's life.

CRUCIFYING SIN

Take up my cross? You mean, like, get crucified? Yeah, sort of.

First, it's not a matter of physical crucifixion. Christ isn't asking you to drag a cross up the biggest hill in your town, then have someone nail you to it. Christ is speaking of a figurative cross, a spiritual crucifixion. This deals with your soul more than your body.

Second, in asking you to take up your cross, Christ is is asking you to live in the ongoing awareness that you already *are* crucified.

What? you ask. *I'm already crucified?*

Yes. Paul puts it this way in Galatians 2:20: "I have been crucified with Christ and I no longer live, but Christ lives in me."

Realize that you already have been crucified. That's an important distinction. If you have to get crucified, your future sounds painful. Some sincere Christian guys vow to do 50 push-ups every time they look lustfully at a beautiful girl—all in an effort to "get crucified." Wow. Those guys have a lot of painful push-ups in their future. But if you already have been crucified, hey, it's already done. You can relax.

COOL. NICE TRUTH. NOW HOW DOES THIS LOOK IN REAL LIFE?

Let's take the looking-lustfully-at-a-beautiful-girl case again. Let's say you're now a freshman at Caltech, and you see a gorgeous girl strutting in front of you. You want to "deny yourself," so you ask, *What should I do, Lord?* Jesus suggests reading the intramural soccer flyer you spotted a few seconds ago. You tell your head to turn, but it doesn't move.

You still want to look at that beautiful girl. It's one thing to know that you're supposed to deny yourself and say yes to Jesus. It's quite another thing to do it. Thanks to Adam, the first sinner, you have something inside that screams for satisfaction, a carnal desire that wants anything other than what God wants. It's called sin, and it still lives in you, even as a believer (Romans 7:17).

That's where taking up your cross comes in. When that beautiful girl crosses your line of vision and those carnal desires kick into lust mode, remind yourself: *I've been crucified with You, Jesus. I'm no longer a slave to sin. Your life is mine. You give me the strength to do what's right. I'm free!*

As you dwell on your crucifixion with Christ, you'll find a growing power within your soul to turn away from those lustful urges. The more you realize that you are dead to Adam, the more you'll appreciate that you are alive in Christ.

Careful, though. Don't quote Galatians 2:20 as if it were a magic wand that will make temptation instantly disappear. It won't. God's Word is not to be used as some weird incantation to—*poof!*—make sin flee. Galatians 2:20 is not a wand; it's truth. Only when truth grips your soul does it become powerful. So, let it take a grip.

Denying yourself and taking up your cross deal with what *not to do.* What about what you *should do?* That's where following Jesus comes in.

FOLLOWING CHRIST ▌ ▌ ▌ ▌ ▌ ▌ ▌ ▌

Jesus returned to heaven 40 days after His resurrection. He's been there ever since, praying for believers and preparing mansions for their arrival. It's true: Jesus, as a man, is not on earth. You can't step into His footprints along the shores of Galilee. But you can still follow Him.

Jesus is here in Spirit. Before Jesus left, He promised: "I will ask the Father, and he will give you another Counselor to be with you forever—the Spirit of truth" (John 14:16-17).

Jesus' Spirit lives in the hearts of believers, counseling, comforting, guiding, and teaching. The Spirit will make it plain what following Jesus looks like—one step at a time. But He doesn't yell. The Spirit speaks in a quiet voice. You've got to stop to listen. Often.

Jesus is present in another sense: the Bible. If you look carefully enough, you'll find Jesus on every page. Think of Isaac on the altar, his life saved by a sacrificial ram (Genesis 22). Jesus is all over that story.

The written Word is Christ, the living Word, in book form. You can't say Jesus is "not around" if you've got a Bible sitting on your dresser.

Be assured: Your Savior wants to make His presence felt. Jesus can be followed. His Spirit is eager to teach you. His Word explains how.

Convinced? Ready for the adventure? You need to be in shape to pull it off.

If you're into physical training, don't stop. Your exercise makes you more alert, more energetic, and quite simply, more alive. But understand this: Your soul needs training even more than your body does. Paul says it this way: "Train yourself to be godly. For physical training is of some value, but godliness has value for all things, holding promise for both the present life and the life to come" (1 Timothy 4:7-8).

You can pump iron your whole life, yet your buff body will still peg out sometime. But an exercised soul will never die. Christians will reap the benefits of spiritual training both here and forever.

Ready to train your inner being? Here are three exercises that will make you spiritually fit:

CHEW ON GOD'S WORD DAILY

Not the paper. The truth it contains. Not with your mouth. With your heart and mind.

Let's consider some rules for physical nutrition: You need food. If you don't get it, you'll crave it. If you don't eat for several days—believe it or not—the hunger pangs will disappear.

If you don't eat for many days, you'll die with a shriveled-up gut. Moreover, it takes time to eat. Eating on the run is not healthy. Don't swallow food whole, or else you may choke. Chew. And give your tongue a chance. Food tastes better that way. The same could be said of spiritual food.

God's Word: You need it desperately. If you don't get it, your soul will crave it. If you don't eat for several days, your spiritual hunger pangs will fade. If you don't eat God's Word for a month, your soul will shrivel.

Eating God's Word takes time. A 30-second glance at the Book won't do much for you. If you bite off too big a chunk, you'll choke. Chew on a small portion of God's Word, nibble it to shreds with your mind. And give your heart a chance. God's Word tastes sweet that way (Psalm 119:103).

God's Word is described as . . .

- milk (1 Peter 2:2)
- meat (Hebrews 5:14, KJV)
- bread (Luke 4:4)
- honey (Psalm 19:9-10)

Makes a guy hungry, doesn't it?

talk to Jesus Daily

Paul was serious when he wrote: "Pray continually" (1 Thessalonians 5:17). Jesus wants you conversing with Him all day long. Sounds impossible, doesn't it? Yet keep these things in mind:

- To pray, you don't need to be in church.
- You don't need to kneel.
- You don't need to do anything with your hands.
- You don't even have to raise your voice.

Jesus can hear you thinking. It's possible, with exercise, to train your mind to "think-talk" with Jesus 24/7 (though it sometimes helps to talk out loud).

While you're showering: *Morning, Friend. What's it mean that I'm crucified with You?*

With your hand on the steering wheel: *Lord, what's the name of that street I'm looking for?*

Even during your graduation speech: *Jesus, I'm about to tell them about You. Give me courage.*

God has made you capable of simultaneously saying one thing with your lips while praying something else with your thoughts. The mind is an amazing thing. Train your brain to pray continually. It's constantly in conversation with itself anyway. With a subtle shift of thinking, a slight pressure of the will, you can direct all your thoughts to Jesus. Instead of thinking, *This hamburger is awesome,* think, *Isn't this hamburger awesome, Jesus?*

The only other option is to just "cerebrate" (talk mentally) with yourself. How boring. Life is way more exciting when you touch base with Jesus all the time. Christ never meant for you to walk the adventure of life alone.

DUMP YOUR SIN LOAD OFTEN

God wants you to dump your load of sin frequently. And dumping sin involves confession, the simple act of admitting to God when you've sinned. "If we confess our sins, he is faithful and just and will forgive us our sins and purify us from all unright-eousness" (1 John 1:9).

Sadly, many Christians don't admit their sin often enough. Ever go to sleep praying, *Lord, if I've sinned today, please forgive me?* Ouch. A few things are definitely wrong with that prayer.

First, unless you've been in a coma all day, you most certainly have sinned—dozens of times. Think of all the selfish thoughts, unkind words, and foolish acts you're capable of in 24 hours. There's no "Lord, if I've sinned . . ." about it. Sin permeates your life like black on coal (1 John 1:8). The more often you learn to confess it, the more you'll be able to enjoy Christ's life.

Second, confession of sin is not something you should do at the end of the day. Sin is best dealt with on the spot. D. L. Moody, a great evangelist, used to toss his hat in the air every time he recognized sin in his life. It was his way of saying, "Thanks, Jesus, for forgiving me again." Kind of quirky, but the man sure understood confession.

Third, if you're going to confess sin, get specific. What action? What word? What thought? What, exactly, did you do wrong?

As you get specific about where you've derailed, God can free you from the guilt associated with each sin. Lame I-probably-sinned-today confessions won't do that for you. Don't go generic when it comes to confessing sin.

Finally, seeing your sin often is not a negative thing. Why? Because confession leads you to this realization: *Lord, I wasn't living Your life right there. Take over again. Let Your life be my life.* What a great desire! So what if you have to pray it 1,000 times a day? That just means you're more sensitive to sin than most. In the meantime, you've had 1,000 reminders that Jesus' life is the only life worth living.

Don't hide from confession. Dump away. Often. It's impossible to wear out 1 John 1:9.

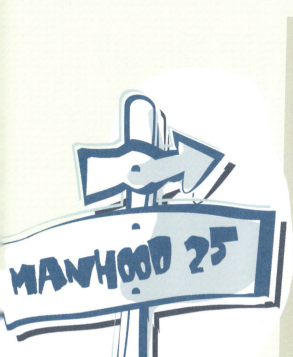

Jesus, the Ultimate Man

This biblical advice, these spiritual exercises, this entire book—all are set before you with one goal in mind: to make you the man God wants you to be. Not a Marlboro man. A real man. A man with no regrets.

The shortest and only road to true manhood is to fix your gaze on the ultimate Man, Jesus Christ. "Let us fix our eyes on Jesus, the author and perfecter of our faith, who for the joy set before him endured the cross, scorning its shame" (Hebrews 12:2).

You think Jesus regrets the cross? No way.

Fix your eyes on Jesus. The longer you look at Christ, the more you'll be like Him.

Dwell on Jesus. The more your soul stares into His eyes, the firmer will be your resolve to follow Him.

Behold the face of Jesus. Gazing at Him, you'll live the adventure He's got in store for you.

Look at Jesus. Be a man. Get a life.

Chapter two: DISCOVER YOUR DESTINY ▌▌▌

The world's movers and shakers each share a secret—a common characteristic that makes them stand out from the crowd: They are obsessed! To be more specific, they are each compelled by THE MAGNIFICENT OBSESSION.

That's right! Planet Earth's most successful men are each guided by a clear personal vision of what Christ wants them to accomplish in life. They've identified their talents and are using them to accomplish God's will. They are men of DESTINY.

Want less stress, more balance, and a more satisfying life? Of course you do. So, stop wasting your time and talent. Clue in to God's will for your life and begin setting life goals. On the pages that follow, we show you how.

getting a clue about god's will ▌ ▌▌▌ ▌▌ ▌ ▌

Okay, let's get real: Figuring out God's will for your life may seem overwhelming at times. It may even feel like some sort of mysterious riddle that's solved by only the holiest members of the Spiritually Elite Club (which completely excludes you, right?).

Guess what? Getting a clue about God's will isn't as hard as you think. It all boils down to *where* you look for answers and who you listen to. It also involves staying in step with God.

BaBy Steps

Your life is filled with lots of simple situations that are easy to figure out—situations that belong in the "baby step" category. Examples of such situations are not choking your little brother when he annoys you and resisting the temptation to cheat on a test.

These kinds of circumstances require a basic knowledge of right and wrong. How do you get this sort of information? Let's explore the options.

Television. Bad choice. Learning right from wrong on the tube puts you in the just-tattoo-"Stupid"-on-my-forehead-and-be-done-with-it category. Too much stuff beamed into your living room on TV goes against Christian values and God's will for our lives. Also, keep in mind that many of the shows you see twist reality. (Not everyone has perfect teeth and a knockout bod.)

Friends. Fair choice. But you have to admit, your friends are walking beside you on the path, not ahead of you. So they probably don't have the kind of experience you need in order to know God's will. Still, don't count them out completely. The Bible says there is wisdom in a multitude of counselors (see Proverbs

15:22). Sometimes, the advice of a good friend can help us make informed choices. Just be sure to choose your friends wisely.

Parents. Good choice. One of God's commandments is to obey and honor your parents (see Ephesians 6:1-2). As you keep maturing, there are some decisions that your parents will want you to make on your own, like where you go to college. But there will be others on which they'll maintain the final word, like whether you can stay out all night with your friends. When it comes to making choices, it's important that you hear your parents out, honor their direction, and obey them when they give an absolute answer. If they make the wrong choice for you, God will deal with them and hold them accountable. You can rest assured that you've done the right thing by obeying. Obeying your parents now brings huge rewards later. It not only pleases God, who promises a blessing (Ephesians 6:2-3), but also your parents will see you as a trustworthy and responsible son. This will pay off when they are willing to trust you to do things you really want to do. If, however, you don't obey them, you will have the full responsibility for your decision on your own head.

Bible. Best choice. All Scripture is "God-breathed" and offers solid advice for just about every situation you'll ever encounter. Through the Word, God teaches, rebukes, corrects, and trains us in righteousness (2 Timothy 3:16).

You'll hear all kinds of reasons why some people favor their feelings over the Bible: "It was written too long ago to be relevant today." "It just doesn't make any sense to me." "No one can know for sure that it's 100 percent accurate."

memorize a promise

"Do you not know?
Have you not heard?
The LORD is the everlasting God,
    the Creator of the ends of the earth.
He will not grow tired or weary,
    and his understanding no one can fathom.
He give strength to the weary
    and increases the power of the weak.
Even youths grow tired and weary,
    and young men stumble and fall;
    but those who hope in the LORD
    will renew their strength.
They will soar on wings like eagles;
    they will run and not grow weary,
    they will walk and not be faint."

—Isaiah 40:28-31

Despite some people's doubts, God's Word is timeless and absolutely, positively accurate in everything He knew was essential for us to know. That's far more trustworthy than our feelings, which change hour by hour. While there is room for debate on secondary issues (such as when the Rapture will occur), there are no discrepancies in God's promises, commands, and warnings. And the fact is, archaeologists and researchers are constantly making new discoveries that confirm the Bible's authority.

man-sized steps

What about life's not-so-easy stuff that we have to figure out? You know, deciding whether or not to go on a missions trip or to give up a certain friendship— or even getting a clue about what God wants us to do with our lives. This is when we begin taking man-sized steps. It's also when the all-important R Factor comes into play. What does the *R* stand for? *Rough? Radical? Run?* Nope. It represents *RELATIONSHIP!*

When you have a close relationship with Jesus, He will tell you HIMSELF what He wants you to do. As we pointed out in chapter one, He communicates with you throughout the day, answering your questions and guiding your steps. You literally walk in His presence minute by minute.

Does God talk to people with an audible voice?
Let's clear up this misconception once and for all. The answer: not usually. In fact, He rarely, if ever, communicates with most of us this way. Instead, the Holy Spirit deals with each human being in a personal and intimate way, convicting, directing, and influencing us.

Think about those times when you faced a temptation of some sort. (Maybe it was lying or stealing or lusting.) Remember how that "something inside" seemed to kick in, telling you to turn away? More than likely, that something was the Holy Spirit directing you to the will of God. Of course, the Lord gave you free will to follow Him or to disobey.

God has promised to speak to our hearts, so we can expect Him to, but He is not compelled to tell us everything we want to know the moment we desire the information.

How can you have a close relationship with God?
First, you must make a personal decision to believe in and follow Jesus. This happens when you realize and become convinced that your sins (which we all have) separate you from Him. This is called *conviction*.

Next, you truly become sorry and choose to turn your back on sin and become a disciple of Jesus. This is called *repentance*.

After that, you offer your whole heart, emotions, decisions, and future to Him. This is called *commitment*.

At this point, hang on to your hat, because the adventure kicks into high gear. When you have an intimate relationship with Jesus, He helps you through difficult situations as they come up. Often, He will even prepare you for them in advance.

How do you determine whether a certain idea is coming from your own head or from God? It takes practice! Sometimes, making a few mistakes helps. Through the years, you slowly begin to recognize the spiritual awareness that all men of God receive when He is speaking to them.

For some people, this awareness takes on a "something's not quite right" feeling when God is trying to get them to avoid a course of action—or when danger is lurking nearby. On the other hand, peace and a sense of confidence are the signs of spiritual awareness that God gives when you're on the right track. And as you grow closer and closer to Him, your instincts will become more sensitive to His influence. Your entire mind and spirit will become more in tune to God, and you'll begin to hear Him more clearly, just as with any good friend.

Does God speak wisdom to you through the voices of other Christians? You bet He does. But you always have to check the advice of others against God's Word. Talking with someone in authority and having him pray as you seek to make decisions are wise steps to take. A godly brother can help you stay accountable to your commitments to God—and he can help you stay on the right track.

BEYOND HIGH SCHOOL: time to set goals ▮ ▮ ▮ ▮ ▮ ▮ ▮ ▮

Most guys go through high school with a survival mentality: *Survive my freshman year. Get past my sophomore year. Grunt out my junior year. Gasp through my senior year.* That's a shortsighted way to live. You don't want to carry that attitude into college, university, or your career. There's a more far-reaching view you need to catch.

THE JUDGMENT SEAT OF CHRIST

You will one day stand there. "For we must all appear before the judgment seat of Christ, that each one may receive what is due him for the things done while in the body, whether good or bad" (2 Corinthians 5:10). If you're a believer, the question won't be: Will you be going to heaven or hell? The question will be: How did you spend the life Jesus gave you? There's no way around it. You'll have to give an answer.

It's time to set some life goals with that day in mind.

Set goals? All I've ever done is score them.

Goals for life are similar to goals in sports. You strive to attain them. There's joy in achieving them. You long to execute them again.

Yes, goals are great. Don't be afraid of setting some for your life.

Create a Life Goal

Remember these three things about a life goal: It's got to be concrete, measurable, and attainable.

A concrete goal is one you can put into words. A vague desire to "be a good Christian" is not very concrete. But "join InterVarsity Christian Fellowship my freshman year" is a solid goal. Goals are most concrete when written down.

A measurable goal is one that allows you to see progress. "Know the Bible from cover to cover" is tough to measure. But "read the New Testament this summer" allows you to mark your progress with that little ribbon dealie in your Bible.

An attainable goal is one that can reasonably be completed. "Lead the world to Christ" is both concrete and measurable but is hardly attainable. "Introduce three people to Jesus before I graduate from college" is a goal that meets all three criteria.

Go for it.

Set Your Goals in Motion

Take an afternoon, a weekend, an hour a day for a month—whatever you need—and pray. Above all, listen to God. Focus on His voice and direction for your life.

Also, begin working out the details by taking these very simple steps:

Dare to dream. No, we're not talking about the kind that's a result of the mouth-wide-open, snoring-on-the-pillow kind of activity. Think about your interests, your desires. Consider the gifts and talents God has given you. Ask God to reveal what His good, pleasing, and perfect will should look like for you (Romans 12:2).

Plot a course. Start writing some concrete, measurable, and attainable goals for your life. Write them in rough, then type them out. You'll want a clean copy to review and rehash on occasion in the future. Setting life goals shouldn't be a one-time affair.

Get some guidance. Talk with your parents or an adult you trust who could possibly become your mentor. Let people know about your dreams and aspirations. Their input can be most valuable in finding the goals that will best shape the man inside you.

And while you're at it, make this your overall target: *When I'm finished life's race, I want to hear Jesus say, "Well done" (Matthew 25:21).* That's concrete. It's a little tough to measure, but it's very attainable.

Get out of survival mode. Become proactive. Set some worthwhile life goals. Get ready for the Judgment Seat.

CHAPTER THREE: SHAPE THE MAN INSIDE ▌▌▌ ▌

You're in the twilight zone between boyhood and manhood. Until now, life's been a blast, a room full of toys, an unending sunset of beach volleyball, a house full of friends in a Nintendo all-nighter. The food's always been there, the sodas are free, the phone's forever paid for, and no one charges rent. Better still, the girls are cute, the money's good, the car will soon be yours, and high school is almost history.

Life is grand, isn't it?

But now it's time to make a few shifts in your thinking. You need a new attitude, a change of gears. Manhood beckons. Where do you begin? We have some ideas.

BOY VERSUS MAN: A SHIFT IN ATTITUDE ▌ ▌▌▌ ▌▌ ▌ ▌

His garage decorated with posters of rippling muscle, Dex Tilford was pumped. The warm-ups had his blood flowing nicely. He felt loose, ready, strong. He lay down on the bench, its cool leather tingling against his bare back. Gazing at the bar above his nose, he took a deep breath and wrapped his hands around the knurled steel.

There was something Dex was supposed to remember.

"Come on, dude. You can do this." Frank Withers stood at the head of the bench, ready to spot.

No use wasting any time. He could do this. Whatever it was he'd forgotten, it would come to him soon enough.

With a grunt, Dex lifted the bar six inches, his arms now fully extended, trembling slightly. He drew another deep breath, then let the bar drop, bouncing it off his chest. He began pressing with all his might.

Through sheer momentum, the first eight inches came easy. After that, the bar crawled slowly upward. Arms shaking, neck straining, eyes bulging, Dex could feel the strength ebb from his body. Just short of the bench rests, the bar stopped rising.

Frank cupped his hands around the bar, ready to grip. "Need a help, dude?"

Dex closed his eyes and shook his head. Then he roared like a wounded bear.

The bar moved.

Three seconds later it was over. The bar lay on its rests. Dex sat up, shoulders flexed, arms held high, fists clenched. Frank was laughing. Dex roared again, this time a bear victorious.

Then his dad came rolling up the driveway in his contractor's rig.

There was something Dex was supposed to remember. It would come to him soon enough. He ran to his father. "Dad, I just pressed 240 pounds!"

"That's great, son." His dad wasn't smiling. A long pause hung in the air. "I was counting on you to meet me at the work site. Remember?"

Oh, gag. Oh, no. His dad had needed help unloading a huge generator. Dex shook his head, eyes on his feet. "I could help now," he suggested.

"Too late. Job's done. Would have been a lot safer with you there."

Dex nodded, wondering why he could never remember stuff.

"Son," his dad continued, one arm around Dex's shoulder, "you've done a lot to get in physical shape. I'm proud of you. But remember: You need to shape the man inside, too."

tuning the 'tude

Manhood calls for a new kind of thinking. Consider these three big ideas.

attitude adjustment no. 1: manhood is a long race

Up until now, every project you've tackled has been comparatively short. But all that's about to change.

Remember those long Saturday mornings, mowing that humongous backyard, the bugs bouncing off your knees? That's nothing. Next summer, you may find yourself fighting clouds of mosquitoes while you trim 206 miles of public trails for Parks and Wildlife.

What about those never-die, 10-page English essays? That's kid's stuff. Writing 206-page business reports may be on your horizon.

Along with manhood comes responsibility. Responsibility is a big word. It makes its appearance in a million places: remembering your word, doing quality research, controlling your emotions, getting to work on time, caring for those under you. The list is long. Any head start you've got on that list is great, but it'll take a man to master responsibility. You've got some major homework ahead of you.

Gear up for the long haul. Hebrews 12:1 puts it this way: "Let us throw off everything that hinders . . . and let us run with perseverance the race marked out for us."

Boyhood was fine until now, but carrying a boy's wimpy attitudes into a man's race will hinder you, big time. And the course God has set is no 40-yard football sprint. It's an ultramarathon. Manhood continues for the rest of your life. Start running, man.

attitude adjustment no. 2: Manhood is a choice

You had no choice to be born a boy. Boyhood came without thinking. It required no act of the will.

Manhood is different. You have to decide to be a man. You've got to exercise your will. A boy eats like a warthog, thinking he's awesome; a man chews his food quietly, conscious of manhood's dignity. A boy lashes back at an insult with screams and fists, his face full of spit and hatred; a man restrains himself, choosing the honor of silence. A boy sees a girl as merely someone to play with; a man decides a woman is worthy of respect, and he acts accordingly. If you don't choose manhood, you'll stay a boy, regardless of how tall you grow. There's an expression that goes like this: "The only differences between men and boys are the cost and size of their toys." That's not a cool message. It reflects the fact that many men grow up in body but not in attitude. Their only goal in life is to have fun. Spiritually speaking, they still crawl around in diapers.

They've never made the choice to be men.

Paul the apostle was a great man because he courageously chose to act like one. He told his readers this: "Be on your guard; stand firm in the faith; be men of courage; be strong" (1 Corinthians 16:13). That's a command. A command requires a choice to obey, a firm act of the will. No lazy minds, weak wills, or flaky halfheartedness allowed.

Paul drew a clear contrast between boys and men with these words: "When I was a child, I talked like a child, I thought like a child, I reasoned like a child. When I became a man, I put childish ways behind me" (1 Corinthians 13:11). Boyhood just happens. Manhood is an attitude, a decision, a step. So put the toys away.

Step into the shoes of a man.

attitude adjustment no. 3: Manhood is God's will for you

Up until now, your assignment from God was fairly simple: "Children, obey your parents in the Lord, for this is right" (Ephesians 6:1).

But you're stepping through a portal now. Once you're on the other side, your parents won't be there to make decisions for you. Life has just gotten more complicated. The challenge of manhood faces you.

A large part of the challenge lies in this question: How are you going to act now that your parents aren't peeping over your shoulder? Are you going to take the godly values they sought to teach you and make them your own? Or will you drop them like hot lava and live like a rebel? Will you choose true manhood, or will you act more like a boy than ever? In one sense, you already know the choice is yours. In another, more awesome sense, the choice has already been made: God has determined to shape the man inside of you. That's His will. The God of the universe has determined for you to "become mature, attaining to the whole measure of the fullness of Christ" (Ephesians 4:13). He's made His decision, and He'll do everything in His power to bring it about (Philippians 1:6).

MANHOOD 25

Think about that. Hard.

It may keep you from hanging out in the shallow end of human existence. It may steer you clear of a weekend binge with guys old enough to buy booze and childish enough to drink it. It may spare God the effort of giving you the spanking of a lifetime.

Spanking of a lifetime? That's right. *I thought I was past that!* Wrong. You may be approaching adulthood, but as a believer, you'll never cease to be God's child. Hebrews 12:5-6 says: "My son, do not make light of the Lord's discipline, and do not lose heart when he rebukes you, because the Lord disciplines those he loves, and he punishes everyone he accepts as a son."

Realize that these words were written to grown-ups. God loves you too much to leave you in diapers. You may choose to keep walking in a boy's shoes, but it will be a painful journey. God wants you to be a man, growing mentally, physically, spiritually, and socially—just like His Son (Luke 2:52).

Ready to grow up? Ready to be a man like Jesus? God is calling.

Without integrity, you don't have much of a future. Proverbs 10:9 says: "The man of integrity walks securely." That's what you want, isn't it? If your desire is to walk through life with confidence, walk like a man, then you need integrity.

What does integrity look like?

- Integrity serves as a guide in life's moral decisions (Proverbs 11:3).

- Integrity hates falsehood in every form (Proverbs 13:5-6).

- Integrity is something to be held on to, even in tough times (Job 2:3).

- Integrity keeps its word even when to do so hurts (Psalm 15:1-4).

- Integrity isn't afraid to run when temptation comes knocking (2 Timothy 2:22).

- Integrity says both yes and no, when each is appropriate, and means what it says (James 5:12).

- Integrity backs up what it says with how it lives (Titus 2:7).

- Integrity understands that all of life is on display before God (1 Kings 9:4).

- Integrity is what God looks for in a man's character (1 Chronicles 29:17).

How do I get integrity?

It happens one choice at a time.

Think of integrity as a tree. Your initial decision not to cross a certain line will plant the seed. "I will not cheat on any of my university assignments, tests, or exams" is a decision that places the acorn of integrity in the soil of your heart. But the process doesn't stop there. You've got to water the seed, fertilize it, make it grow.

Every time you keep a promise, even though it costs you great effort, your integrity is watered. Every time you choose to tell the truth when tempted to lie, you fertilize your integrity.

Every time you treat a beautiful young lady with respect, your integrity grows. It will start out as a small root, where only God can see it. But over time, your integrity will stand tall, its branches wide. People will notice. Standing in the shade of your integrity, they'll say, "He's cool. You can count on that guy." Word will get around.

Once word gets around, you've got it. Integrity is about reputation. It's not a hidden characteristic; it's a public thing.

But integrity is also a fragile thing. One act of deception can fell your good reputation like a chain saw. After one evening of heavy petting, your integrity falls like deadwood. Integrity is not so much about getting it; it's about keeping what you already have. Keep your integrity, and it will grow. Fail to keep it, and it's a stump. Another shoot can grow from that stump, but it'll be a long time before anyone sees a tree again.

How important is integrity?

While waiting in the cafeteria line, two older executives discussed a promising young newcomer to

the company. The object of their discussion stood several people ahead of them, far enough so that he couldn't hear them but near enough so that they could observe him. As they spoke, the young man hid a package of crackers under his plate so that he wouldn't have to pay for it. He saved himself 25 cents. The one executive turned to the other and said, "No integrity. No future."

As a follower of Christ, you have a future with far greater potential than merely a high-paying executive slot. You're living for the King of Kings, the One who kept His integrity right to the cross. The rewards for integrity on earth last forever in heaven.

Yeah, integrity is important. So get it. And once you've got it, don't sell out on it. Integrity has its rewards, but like truth, it is priceless (Proverbs 23:23).

Choose manhood. Get integrity. Shape the man inside.

part two: **BODY BASICS**

CHAPTER FOUR

911—HELP! WHAT'S GOIN' ON DOWN THERE?!

For some guys, the subjects we're about to tackle are nothing new. You've already endured that sweaty-hands, dry-mouth, birds-and-the-bees conversation with Mom and Dad. Besides, you've been a teenager for a few years, so you're cruising into manhood without a single bump in the road. (Yeah, right!)

But for other boys, puberty is a brand-spankin' NEW experience—especially all the insane stuff happening to your body. Hello, God! Did You make a mistake here—or what?!

You've got questions. Tons of them. And we've got answers. Regardless of your situation—old pro who needs a refresher course or frantic new guy who desperately needs some honest guidance—read on and learn some body basics. We think you'll figure out that (1) God didn't goof, and (2) the kid who is under construction right now is transforming into a pretty cool man.

BODY WARP: THE INCREDIBLE MORPHING KID

It's sort of a strange word, but what is puberty (pronounced pyoo-ber-tee), and how does a guy know when it happens?

There are many different ways of knowing when puberty hits. Often you receive a letter from the National Department of Puberty. Other times, the announcement comes through a school counselor who shouts your name over the intercom with an urgent message: "Report to my office immediately for official puberty notification!" And then, sometimes, the only way you can tell is by clicking on the tube and waiting for Regis Philbin to announce your name as the next contestant on *Who Wants to Be a Man?*

Okay . . . seriously, puberty doesn't happen overnight. It isn't like waking up one morning with a 102-degree fever. (Although, on some days, it may feel that way.) Puberty is a gradual process that has probably already begun in you. It marks a turning point: the stage of your life when you begin the journey from boyhood to manhood.

Growth spurt. The word *spurt* describes a short burst of activity, something that happens in a hurry. And that's exactly what takes place with the onset of puberty. Your body begins to grow—fast! (Some guys gain more than four inches in height in a single year.) Yet all this growth during puberty will be the last time in your life that your body will get taller. When you finish your growth spurt, you will be at your adult height.

Body changes. Keep checking the mirror, and you'll notice that you're literally getting a new body, a new look, during the next few years: muscle growth, new hair scattered all over in some very adult places, not to mention the curse of growing up—ZITS!

Occasionally, you'll wish you could hide behind a sign that reads "STAY AWAY—UNDER CONSTRUCTION!" But try to be patient because, when the manhood morphing process is over, you're going to like the new you.

Sexual awakening. You've probably noticed a strong appetite for sex—like, duh! And you're certainly aware of one of the more embarrassing aspects of being a guy: frequent erections. When you have an erection, your penis fills with blood and becomes hard. This usually happens when you are sexually excited, but it's also normal to get erections for no reason at all (called spontaneous erections). Rest assured, they're usually not as noticeable to other people as they are to you.

Adolescence. This refers to the gap between the time when you are fully grown and biologically mature and the point when our culture says you're ready to embrace the world as a responsible man—enter the work force, marry, and take responsibility for a family of your own as well as for your career.

Five Stages of Puberty in Guys

1 Ages 9-12. Inside your body, male hormones are becoming active. They travel through the blood and give the testes the signal to begin the production of testosterone (pronounced teh-stahs-teh-rown) and sperm. Translation: When these hormones finish their work, you'll no longer think girls have cooties. (In fact, you'll probably find yourself very intrigued by cooties!)

2 Ages 9-15. Your testicles grow and begin hanging lower. Pubic hair appears at the base of your penis. Testosterone begins to transform the shape of your body. Your muscles grow bigger in your chest and shoulders. Cool!

3 Ages 11-16. Your penis gets longer and a little wider, and pubic hair gets darker and coarser. Facial and underarm hair may develop, as well as hair on your legs. Your voice may begin to lower in pitch and may even "crack" at times—usually the *wrong* times. (During this stage, you'll find it much more difficult to sing with the Muppets, especially if you're trying to perform Miss Piggy's part.)

4 Ages 11-17. You'll notice another growth spurt in your penis, which gets wider and longer. More body hair appears and takes on an adult texture. Okay, here comes the semi-scary part: You'll encounter your first ejaculation. You may actually be awakened some night by what is called a "wet dream" (an ejaculation of semen from your penis). This can feel a little weird—probably not the kind of thing you'll want to share in youth group. But don't worry, it's totally normal.

5 Ages 14-18. Your body will reach full adult height and physique. Pubic hair spreads to your thighs and up toward your belly. Chest hairs may appear, and shaving is a must unless you want a beard.

sexual appetite ▌▌▌▌ ▌▌ ▌ ▌

It's easy to look at sex as intercourse and say, "I won't do that." What's more difficult is to look at the process that leads up to sex. But overlooking that buildup is like looking at a raging inferno and saying, "I'll stay away from there," while you gather matches, gasoline, and oil-soaked rags. Those ingredients may be pretty harmless on their own, but put 'em all together and you've got some serious potential for disaster.

The pathway to sex is similar. God made our bodies to get revved up and accelerate toward sex. It's true for both men and women, although the timetable and sequence can be different. You may have already experienced it. You start holding hands. It's exciting at first, but then you want your arm around the girl. Cool. Next comes kissing. That might start with a kiss on the cheek or an innocent peck on the lips, but then it builds to passionate, open-mouthed, prolonged kissing.

Are you getting the picture? Your sexual appetite is powerful. What's more, sexual arousal builds. It's supposed to. That process is part of the connection of sex. The further down the road you get, the harder it is to stop.

An important part of *beating* temptation is *avoiding* temptation. You can't give in to a temptation that isn't there. How does that apply to you? Two ways.

1. Set clear boundaries now about what you will or won't do physically. Pray about them. Write them down. Share them with a friend.

2. Be patient. You've got plenty of time until marriage and sex. So what's the big hurry to get physically connected? It takes a lot of self-control to say "Whoa!" once your body's flame is burning. Don't fan the fire and make it tougher than it has to be.

to fellow Breakaway Readers

I'm writing to you about one of the most important decisions you will ever make—saving your body for your future wife.

About a year ago I failed God by not staying pure. At the time, I was reckless and really didn't care what happened to my life or anyone else's. I ended up having sex and tossing aside my virginity like an old rag. Even though God has forgiven me, it'll be a long time before I forgive myself (if ever).

I lost something precious—something I can never get back.

Listen, guys, I wish I'd never had sex. I'm more ashamed of this than anything I've ever done in my life. Stay pure.

—Daniel

masturbation ▌ ▎ ▎ ▎ ▌▌ ▎ ▌

There, we said it. We know you're thinking about it. We know you've probably done it.

No, we're not psychic. We're guys too.

A fairly recent poll found that 88 percent of college men had masturbated at least once. The joke is that the other 12 percent are probably lying.

You are not alone.

But if everybody's doing it, why is no one talking about it? Despite our culture's preoccupation with sex, our sexuality and sexual development are very private, personal matters. And historically, there have been a lot of myths and scary facts floating around, or even being taught, about masturbation. But maybe the biggest silencer is guilt. Satan loves to heap it on, and he'd love to use it to drive a wedge between you and God.

will masturbating hurt me?

There is no scientific evidence that masturbating will hurt your body. It does not cause blindness, weakness, dehydration, and mental or other physical problems. If it did, there would be far more blind, wimpy, dried-up, simpleminded, sick men.

god and man on masturbation

What does the Bible say about masturbation? Good question. Nothing. Some have taught that the story of Onan in Genesis 38:8-10 is an example against masturbation, but many Bible scholars and Christian leaders believe that the story has nothing to do with masturbation. Instead, Onan displeased God because he refused to obey the law of taking his dead brother's wife as his own.

Many Christians disagree about masturbation. Those who believe it's wrong often point to lust and pornography in their reasoning. Those who believe it's a normal part of adolescence point to the Bible's silence on the subject as an indicator that it's not a big deal to God. Ultimately, no one can say for sure exactly how God views masturbation.

don't worry about it

If you don't struggle with masturbation or don't do it, great. There's nothing wrong with you, either. Every individual is different; the same is true sexually. But if you do masturbate, relax. During the sexual development of your teen years, the urge can seem almost uncontrollable, but God understands. Some guys have literally thrown away their faith over the cycle of broken promises to God that they'll never masturbate again. But it's just not worth it. God doesn't reject you, no matter how many times you've broken your promise to Him.

Watch the Danger Spots

Being consumed by anything can be dangerous, and masturbation is no exception. It can be a problem if it becomes an obsession, something that controls you. Excessive masturbation can be defined as an activity that occurs several times a day for a prolonged period of time.

How do you know if you have a problem? Ask yourself these questions:

- Is masturbation all I think about?
- Have I been doing it multiple times a day, every day, for months in a row?
- Do I regularly refuse to do fun activities I like with other people so that I can be alone to masturbate?

If you've got a couple of yeses, talk with someone about your patterns. Try your dad or a male youth pastor, and go over this chapter of the book together. It'll seem tough, but remember, they're guys too. They've more than likely faced the struggles of masturbation.

The biggest danger comes when you masturbate while fantasizing about a specific girl. At that point it has become sheer lust, and it displeases God. See chapter eight about that.

So, What Should I Do—or Not Do?

We're not recommending that you masturbate. If it's not an issue and you don't feel the need for it, great. If you do masturbate, don't beat yourself up over it and certainly don't let guilt drive you away from God. Just be sure to avoid the danger zones.

Either way, talk the issue over honestly with God and with a godly older man—and keep pursuing purity. Getting past Satan's shameful accusations and realizing that you're not alone will make a huge difference.

CHAPTER FIVE: I'M BECOMING a man— BUT am I normal?

One word best describes your life right now: CHANGE! Your body is literally a chemical laboratory that's exploding with all kinds of new activity. And with all these changes going on inside (and outside), you can't help asking yourself, Is this normal? Am I normal?

Maybe you've sprouted three inches above everyone else your age. Or maybe they did the growing, which makes you feel like a shrimp. Is this normal?

Perhaps you've just entered junior high and your body is already beginning to look more like a man's, complete with a beard that needs maintenance every morning. Or it could be that you're well into high school (with an eye on college), yet—unlike some of the other guys your age—you still have that annoying "baby face" that grandmothers can't resist pinching every time they lay eyes on you. Is this normal?

Despite all the different body shapes and sizes you see at school or in the locker room, rest assured: YOU'RE NORMAL!

On the following pages, we'll tackle the major questions that teen guys have about their entry into manhood, and we'll arm you with tips that will help you deal with all the changes. We'll even clear the air about what makes a man a REAL MAN.

WHaT IS "normal"?

Even though this manhood morphing process is a normal part of growing up, how can you be sure that everything that's going on is truly normal?

Let's define the word *normal*. Despite the rigid conformity codes imposed by cliques, *normal* really can't be synonymous with the word *same*. If it were, the planet would be incredibly abnormal, right? (Imagine how weird it would be sharing Earth with cookie-cutter clones.) Instead, everybody's different.

Some people are tall, while others are short. Some have broad shoulders, while others are lean. (You get the picture.)

So, different really is normal. God created you to be a unique individual, and He even put you on a developmental schedule that may be different from some guys—but that's just right for you.

GOD MADE US DIFFERENT!

How different are people? Get this: The world is populated with . . .

- five major races (Australoid, Capoid, Caucasian, Oriental, Negro)
- seven colors (black, white, yellow, red, tan, brown, gray)
- 432 major people groups
- 9,000 distinct ethnic groups

Incredible, isn't it? God didn't fill the planet with clones, so why let peer pressure turn you into one? Here's the most awesome news of all: Despite the billions of men, women, and children who populate Earth, Christ shows no favoritism. He loves each one as if that person were the only one!

I'M TOO SHORT

I'm shorter than most guys my age. Do I have any hope of growing taller?

Believe it or not, your feet are an excellent predictor for your height. Occasionally there's an exception, but the longer the shoe size in a boy's early teen years, the taller the man is going to be.

Also, if you haven't yet completed your growth spurt (see chapter four for details), there's a solid chance that you'll get taller. The rule about when you reach your adult height is this: You'll keep growing taller until your beard gets bristled and feels like sandpaper within 24 hours of shaving.

The fact is, your transformation from boy to man is a hereditary thing. You'll grow and develop at a similar rate as your parents. So, you may want to sit down with your father and ask a few questions: "Dad, how old were you when you got taller? At what age did puberty hit? Did you ever feel as if you were smaller than other guys your age? How'd you handle it?" You might also consider talking to your family doctor during your next physical.

Regardless of your size, others will accept you because of your *attitude,* not your *altitude.* It's best to focus your energy on growing the man inside: your values, how you treat other people, and especially how much you imitate Christ.

YOU

ME

? I'M TOO SKINNY

My body is way too skinny—not muscular like some guys. Is there anything I can do to build it up?

!

Your body is the product of both genetics (which you can't alter) and lifestyle (which you can). While you can't work yourself into any body configuration you choose, every teen guy has many more options than he realizes. Inbred limitations can't be totally overcome, but they can definitely be overshadowed: Even the most average person can sculpt a better body from his particular genetic clay. But it takes some dedication.

By working out and getting some exercise on a daily basis, you can build up your body. And when you look your best, you feel good, too.

The fact is, your body likes to work. God designed it that way. It wants to be strong and fit. If you choose to work out and get any kind of exercise, you're doing a great thing for yourself. The results will come if you stick with it. That's a fact.

But beware: It's a big mistake to become obsessed with building the perfect body. Your goal shouldn't be to look like the school quarterback—or anyone else. Instead, you should take what you have and make it the best it can be. And when that's your goal, you'll feel 100 percent better about yourself.

I DON'T HAVE ANY PUBIC HAIR

I'm 15, and I don't have any hair down there. In fact, my face and body still look like those of an elementary school kid, not a young man. Am I okay?

Yes, you are okay. As we pointed out at the beginning of this chapter, each guy has his own *normal* biological timetable for development. Your sexual changes are triggered by a tiny organ near the center of your brain that operates like an internal command center. It's called the *pituitary gland,* and despite being the size of a small bean, it stores the blueprint for your entire body. Your very own manhood morphing process is controlled by the pituitary gland.

In his book *Preparing for Adolescence* (Regal Books), Dr. James Dobson explains it this way: "At just the right time [the pituitary gland] will send out chemical messengers, called *hormones,* which will tell the rest of the glands in your body, 'Get moving, it's time to grow up.' "

While it's frustrating to mature later than some of your peers, understand that you won't remain trapped in a child's body forever. Sometime soon your hormones will get their marching orders, and you'll begin the awesome transformation from boy to man.

In the meantime, here are a few body facts to think about:

Guys having Asian or American Indian genes tend not to become as hairy as those of European or African descent.

You'll grow and develop at a similar rate as your parents when they experienced puberty. As we mentioned earlier, consider sharing your concerns with your dad or family physician.

God created you, which means you are a valuable, one-of-a-kind masterpiece. The Bible says you are "fearfully and wonderfully made":

> For you created my inmost being;
>   you knit me together in my mother's womb.
> I praise you because I am fearfully and
>   wonderfully made;
>   your works are wonderful,
> I know that full well.
> My frame was not hidden from you
>   when I was made in the secret place.
> When I was woven together in the depths of
>   the earth, your eyes saw my
>   unformed body.
> All the days ordained for me
>   were written in your book
>   before one of them came to be.
>   —Psalm 139:13-16

CAUTION UNDER CONSTRUCTION

I'm not circumcised

What exactly is the purpose of circumcision, and why is this done to so many guys? I'm not like them, and that makes me scared to take a shower during gym class. I'm afraid the other boys will think I'm weird.

Circumcision is the surgical removal of the foreskin, or *prepuce*—a flap of skin located at the head of the penis. This is done to many boys shortly after birth because it is believed to be an effective way of keeping the penis clean. However, it was originally a Jewish rite that was performed as a sign of reception into their faith.

Regardless, understand this: It's not abnormal to be uncircumcised. Also, circumcision makes no difference in how the penis functions. Yet uncircumcised boys and men should wash under the foreskin every day in order to keep the area clean.

MY ERECTIONS EMBARRASS ME

I get erections all the time, which is really embarrassing. I not only get them while talking to girls, but—I'm ashamed to admit—I've even gotten an erection while taking a shower during gym class. Is this normal? Or am I struggling with some kind of sexual perversion?

During puberty and the early teen years, guys get lots of erections, often for no reason at all. It's totally normal, so don't freak out. And chances are, they're not noticeable to other people.

Getting them at awkward moments can feel devastating—especially when you're in the locker room, wearing nothing but your birthday clothes! But understand this: (1) You're not alone; it happens to many guys. (2) You're not weird. And (3) you're certainly NOT perverted or homosexual. God did not create you that way.

The fact is, your body is racing with hormones as well as all kinds of emotions and desires. For the next few years, it will seem as if the slightest thought or activity can cause an erection. The best thing you can do is ignore it and concentrate on something else until it passes.

I don't act very macho

I guess you could call me the more sensitive type. I'm not really into sports or the outdoors, and I prefer stuff like reading, writing, and art. But some guys make fun of me and call me a sissy. Is it okay if a guy doesn't act real macho?

The best person you can be is . . . YOU! If you're a skilled athlete, then be an athlete. If you're a talented artist, then be an artist. But don't waste your energy trying to be macho. You really can be sensitive and be a man.

Think about it: Why should you have to climb Mount Everest or become your school's MVP or act like Mr. Teenage Studmaster just to prove your manhood? What's more, isn't it crazy to force yourself to be someone you're not or to live up to the crowd's impossible definition of what it means to be a man?

Yet that's exactly what many guys do—even Christian teens. They hide their emotions behind a tough male armor, never flinching, always fearing humiliation from their peers. Instead, be smart and be yourself.

One last thing: If you think girls are interested only in macho-acting, muscle-bound jocks, think again! Listen to what 16-year-old Stacie of Boulder, Colorado, has to say:

"I've been attracted to both jocks and artistic types. Every girl is different, and each one has individual things that they find attractive in a guy. But girls, for the most part, care most about a guy's heart, as well as his personality. These are the qualities that matter most."

I'm not ready to date

? All my friends are girl-crazy. Not me. In fact, I'm not really interested in dating or having a girlfriend right now. Is there something wrong with me?

! It feels weird to be left out, especially when all your friends are comfortable with something that may give you anxiety (like dating). First, we want to get something straight with you: Being "girl-less" does not mean you're any less of a guy. Despite what your friends are doing, it's okay to not date. The truth is, you're not weird at all!

When it comes to the whole guy/girl thing, each person is on a different time line. In fact, some teens have decided not to date at all.

Listen to what Josh, an 18-year-old from El Paso, Texas, has to say: "I don't believe in dating. I've been ridiculed by Christians and non-Christians about this, but I don't need any more temptations in my life. I'm not ready to get married, so why even flirt with the idea? God is the Creator of the universe, so it's nothing for Him to send me my true wife when the time is right."

Daniel, 16, of Charlottesville, Virginia, has another view: "Right now I think it's better to go out in groups. It's safer and it's more fun. Going out one-on-one can be boring. I think of girls as just friends."

Our advice: Take your time. Dating is a decision that's up to you, your parents, and the Lord.

One more thing: If you feel comfortable doing this, let your friends know that you've decided to go slow with relationships. And when the topic turns to dating, take charge and change it. If that's impossible, take a deep breath and remind your brain of what we said earlier: Being girl-less doesn't make you any less of a guy.

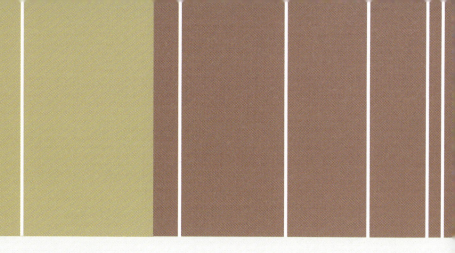

? I constantly think about sex

I constantly think about sex and have thoughts about girls that I know I shouldn't. Am I okay? How can I deal with this?

Your attraction to girls is totally normal and God-given. That's right—it's all *His* idea. Despite how the media distorts it, sex really isn't some kind of dirty three-letter word. It's actually a gift—an awesome part of your life that you should never be ashamed of. (See chapter eight for more about sex.)

In fact, God wants you to have self-control now so that you can enjoy *good sex* in the future—with your wife in a lifelong Christian marriage. What's more, He wants you to behave like a gentleman and to have the utmost respect for girls and women. "Flee the evil desires of youth, and pursue righteousness, faith, love and peace, along with those who call on the Lord out of a pure heart" (2 Timothy 2:22).

But let's face it: Pursuing purity isn't easy. Here are some tips on how you can stay cool when the heat is on.

Keep in mind that sex is only a drive. It's NOT a NEED. Oxygen, food, and water are needs. Flip open a newspaper and read the obituary section. You'll quickly notice that the cause of death is never "lack of sex."

Understand that needs must be satisfied; drives must be directed. No matter how strong the urge to explore further, the good news is that you can control it. (That is, with Christ's help.) A promise in 1 Corinthians 10:13 basically says this: "There is no temptation that can tackle us if we let Jesus do the blocking."

Determine to change the way you think about females. When you look at a girl in sexual terms, catch yourself and train your mind to view her in nonsexual ways.

Watch what you put in your brain. Don't take in movies, pictures, or songs that feed your fantasies. While we can't always stop thoughts from coming into our minds, we can make sure that we don't entertain racy images and invite them to spend the night. Second Corinthians 10:5 tells us what to do: "We take captive every thought to make it obedient to Christ."

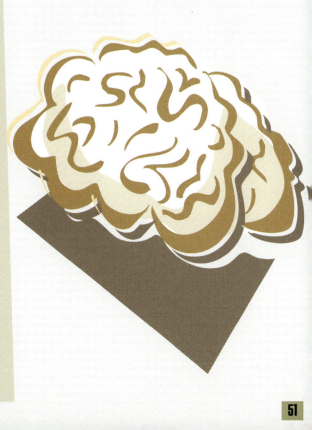

? sometimes I look at pornography

Sometimes I look at pornography as I masturbate. Is this wrong?

! Pornographic material (even if the women aren't completely naked) is the biggest danger surrounding masturbation and one to avoid at all costs. It can damage you mentally and emotionally—even for the rest of your life. Those seductive visual images can literally become stuck in your brain. The lies of porn—that women should look perfect (by the way, they're all airbrushed so they look perfect even though they're not), be constantly turned on, and exist solely as your sexual plaything—can warp your thinking and cause problems in your future marriage and relationships with women in general. It can even become an addiction, just like any drug, only this one eats up your heart and mind. Got any porn? Get rid of it—fast. (For more about the dangers of porn, see chapter nineteen.)

What if I'm gay?

I've been having a really tough struggle with certain things lately, and I just want to get to the bottom of it all. I'd like to know the truth about homosexuality—and the issue of two or more guys masturbating together (even having sex with each other).

I want to know the truth on these matters and where I should stand as a Christian. What does God have to say about these things? How can I combat my feelings, desires, and fantasies?

We respect your courage as well as your desire for the truth.

You asked if it is a sin to masturbate with other guys or to engage in anal or oral sex with them. Our answer is pretty clear: Yes, these activities are sinful and should be avoided by Christian young men.

In the Bible (1 Corinthians 6:18-20, to be exact) we read: "Flee from sexual immorality. All other sins a man commits are outside his body, but he who sins sexually sins against his own body. Do you not know that your body is a temple of the Holy Spirit, who is in you, whom you have received from God? You are not your own; you were bought at a price. Therefore honor God with your body."

Several verses earlier, in 1 Corinthians 6:9-10, we read: "Do not be deceived: Neither the sexually immoral nor idolaters nor adulterers nor male prostitutes nor homosexual offenders nor thieves nor the greedy nor drunkards nor slanderers nor swindlers will inherit the kingdom of God." Romans 1:18-32 has a lot to say on these issues.

Here are some highlights: "[Men] exchanged the truth of God for a lie. . . . Men also abandoned natural relations with women and were inflamed with lust for one another. Men committed indecent acts with other men, and received in themselves the due penalty for their perversion" (Romans 1:25-27).

We could continue with more scriptures, but we think you get the picture.

As we've mentioned earlier in this chapter, God designed sex to be experienced between a husband and a wife in marriage. Anything other than His awesome design is against His will. And trust us, living apart from His will can be pretty miserable. Maybe not at first, but eventually.

You said that you wanted the truth about sex and that you wanted to know where you should stand as a Christian. Everything we wrote is the truth of God as we know it.

We sincerely hope that you will follow God's design for sex. We realize that it can get pretty confusing, especially with the powerful sexual desires that you are dealing with. But understand this: Jesus Christ loves you and cares deeply about your struggles. (He understands them better than you do.) He will help you. As I mentioned earlier, PRAY. Tell Him everything you're feeling and ask Him for help. Jesus forgives and heals.

One more thing: Is there a trusted Christian adult, such as your father or your pastor, you can talk to about all of this? We urge you to do so. Don't carry this alone. Get the advice of a Christian brother.

CHAPTER SIX: BUFFING UP YOUR BOD

As we discussed in chapter four, your whole body is transforming right before your eyes. And that means you'll occasionally wish you could hide behind a sign that reads "STAY AWAY—UNDER CONSTRUCTION!"

Hang in there, because you're gonna like the finished product. In the meantime, here's a solid plan for an acne attack—along with some health-conscious tips that'll help you buff up your bod.

DEFEATING THE ZIT ZOMBIE

Acne, blemishes, pimples, whiteheads, blackheads, nature bumps, zits—regardless of what you call them, they all amount to one thing: misery.

Sometime during the night, you get zapped by the dreaded Zit Zombie. The timing is bad, as usual, and now the situation looks hopeless. But worst of all, you are convinced that your social life is over—FOR GOOD!

Don't lose hope, because you aren't alone. Companies that make acne products claim that more than 17 million North American teenagers and young adults go through anguish every day over blemishes.

How do they know this? Easy—the ZIA (Zit Intelligence Agency) has attached a camera behind your bathroom mirror. They've photographed those desperate grimaces on your face each time you spot a zit. (We're joking, okay?)

In truth, it's estimated that more than $1 million a day is spent in drugstores on acne remedies. Some of the biggest sellers include Oxy Clean Pads, Oxy 10, Stri-Dex Medicated Pads, Neutrogena Antiseptic Cleanser, and Clearasil Vanishing Lotion.

Many other teens follow a daily regimen of oral antibiotics, restrictive diets, and even sunlamps. The bottom line: Nearly every adolescent guy and girl is plagued with pimples to some degree. Considering this, are there success secrets for treating acne? Is there a cure? Yes and no.

We got our hands on tons of information about this age-old dilemma, and we even picked the brain of a dermatologist (a doctor who treats acne). Here's what we learned.

THE PROBLEM: a case of growing up ▮▮▮▮ ▮▮ ▮

A majority of teen guys suffer from a variety of acne types, each occurring for different reasons. But the most common kind is known as *acne vulgaris*. (Appropriate name, right?!)

This condition can develop on almost any part of your body but usually shows up on the face, neck, chest, and back.

What causes it? Eons before zits appear on your skin (okay, maybe not that long ago), trouble has been building up beneath the surface—in your hair follicles and oil glands (also called *pores*).

Cells that line a follicle are constantly being replaced. They mix with a sticky oil (called *sebum*), work their way to the skin's surface, and are washed away.

For reasons highlighted below, the process sometimes goes berserk. Cells, oil, and bacteria stick together and form a plug that clogs up the pore. As more and more oil gets blocked, the follicle swells and forms what is known as a whitehead or blackhead. (In other words, a zit.)

According to Dr. Ron Johnson, a Colorado Springs dermatologist who helps a lot of teens with acne, all this happens because of three things:

Hormones: "These are very active in a teen guy. If they're not, then something is wrong. So the appearance of acne actually means you're normal and that you're becoming a man."

Heredity: "Adam and Eve must have both had acne, since we're all descendants of that line. But when there's a strong hereditary component—like when Mom and Dad have scarred faces from pimples— that's a sign that you'll have trouble too."

Stress: "An emotional time at home, breaking up with your girlfriend, a test, the drive it takes to compete in an important game—each of these stressful situations can result in acne flare-ups. Beware."

While you can't stop all this from happening, you can do some troubleshooting to lessen the problem and make it more bearable.

THE SOLUTION: grooming game plan

WASH DAILY

Morning and night is best, using a medicated soap designed to treat acne. Also, try a mild abrasive, such as Pernox or a Buf-Puf pad. But be careful. These products can cause irritation if used improperly.

USE A PRODUCT CONTAINING BENZOYL PEROXIDE

These medications effectively attack the germs that cause unsightly inflammation.

SEE A DERMATOLOGIST

He or she may recommend a daily regimen, using prescription products such as T-Stat, Cleocin-T, or Retin-A. PhisoHex, a special soap, is another effective weapon in the war against acne. For severe cases, dermatologists sometimes pull out a big gun: a miracle drug called Accutane.

HANDLE STRESS

When you encounter a nerve-bending time (like finals), it's possible to avoid an acne outbreak by taking a few precautions:

- Have a pep talk with yourself and RELAX!
- Get enough sleep each night.
- Eat healthfully.
- Exercise daily.

The most important treatment Dr. Johnson gives his patients is a word of encouragement: "You're normal! People expect you to have a few pimples—you're not a leper," he points out. "Of course, that's easier to say than believe when you're in the trenches. But hang in there; acne is a normal part of growing up."

MUSCLE—BUILDING NUTRITION ▮ ▮ ▮ ▮ ▮ ▮ ▮ ▮

Fact: Eating the right food (and staying clear of the bad stuff) is important for guys your age.

Fact: Some guys don't realize that what they're shoving in their face may zap their energy and cause a visit from the Zit Zombie. So the next time you eat three burgers, a sack of chips, and a quart of chocolate milk for lunch, don't blame us the next morning. (You were warned!)

Fact: Your body's a machine. The harder you work it and the better fuel you put in it, the stronger and

bigger it gets. But building your body into a Maserati isn't easy; muscles don't always build quickly. (You've probably already figured that out.)

Genetics has a lot to do with it. Some guys just develop muscles faster. God designed their bodies that way. If you haven't hit puberty yet, that will work against you. But your lifestyle can also contribute to muscle development. Proper nutrition and sleep play important roles in gaining a healthy body.

BODYBUILDING facts

Water is the most important nutrient in your body. So, put down the soda pop and Gatorade and drink some H_2O. A 165-pound athlete is composed of 50 quarts of water. Muscles are three-quarters water. Your bones are one-quarter water.

Your body builds muscle only during rest and sleep. Seven and a half to nine and a half hours of sleep a night are recommended.

The best diet for athletes: whole grains and vegetables, especially brown rice, rolled oats, soybeans, and black-eyed peas. Sorry, corn chips and oatmeal cookies don't qualify. Eating three solid meals a day is good advice.

Protein is the building block of muscle. Foods low in fat and high in protein are great muscle builders. Some of the best foods are egg whites, grilled flounder and orange roughy, tuna, and roasted skinless turkey and chicken. On the other hand, stay away from beefsteak, pork loin, bacon, and butter. Fast food can be bad for the body. Lean, muscular bodies demand lean food. Fast food tends to have a lot of fat. Fat should make up about 20 percent of your diet.

- McDonald's french fries are almost half fat, but the McLean Deluxe is only 28 percent fat.

- Arby's regular roast beef sandwich is 43 percent fat, but the roast beef light deluxe is 31 percent fat.

- Burger King's Whopper is 53 percent fat, but the chunky chicken salad without dressing is 25 percent fat.

- Taco Bell's regular taco is 54 percent fat, but the bean burrito is 28 percent fat.

- Boston Market's one-quarter, white meat chicken with skin is 48 percent fat, but without the skin and wing it is only 22 percent fat.

There is no substitute for proper nutrition. Protein and vitamin supplements are expensive and not necessary or helpful for teens. In fact, if the calories from a weight-gain shake aren't burned, they're stored as fat. Plus, some doctors say creatine phosphate—a popular muscle-building supplement—can increase weight but also increases muscle cramps and heat-related reactions.

Stay balanced. Even if you take supplements and eat the perfect diet, it's important to remember what Dr. Michael Colgan says in his book *Optimum Sports Nutrition:* "Protein intake doesn't control muscle growth, but rather the trauma of intense exercise. No one ever grew an ounce of muscle from simply gulping protein. Muscles grow from pushing poundage—period."

BODYBUILDING Basics

To some guys, a well-carved chest is like a billboard that shouts "STRONG BODY." But before you knock yourself out to prime those pecs, don't neglect the muscles in your arms, shoulders, and back. Otherwise, you could end up with an impressive chest but a shoulder that aches after five seconds of air hockey.

Remember: The results won't come overnight, especially if you don't lift weights on a regular basis. Building an awesome body takes discipline, commitment, and time.

Workout Reminders

- Before jumping into exercise, don't forget to stretch properly and warm up the muscles you will be using.

- Do these exercises at least three days a week (not in a row).

- Breathe properly. Exhale on the exertion phase (when your muscle contracts) and inhale on the relaxation phase (when your muscle relaxes).

- We recommend that you see a medical doctor before you begin a workout program.

Workout Questions

How old should I be before I start weightlifting?
According to the professional trainers we've talked to, boys of any age can work out with weights as long as they don't try to be Mr. Macho and lift too much. Start with light weights and make sure there isn't any undue strain on your joints.

Which is better: barbells or weight machines?
Die-hard weight lifters will tell you that barbells are the way to go. Machines, however, are safer and easier to use. Why? (1) Since the bars and handles at weight stations are attached to the machines, you don't have to worry about balancing the weights, which means (2) less muscle fiber is placed under stress and (3) you can work out alone—without the assistance of a spotter.

But if you have the time, the proper training (like from a coach or your dad), as well as a workout partner, exercising with barbells is the preferred way of getting into shape.

Try stretch bands, too, especially when you are away from home and need to rely on handy, portable equipment.

What are the best exercises for teen guys?
A workout should include stretching, running (or jogging), sit-ups, pull-ups, bench press, military press, dumbbell curls, and squats. You can achieve much strength and muscular size with these simple exercises.

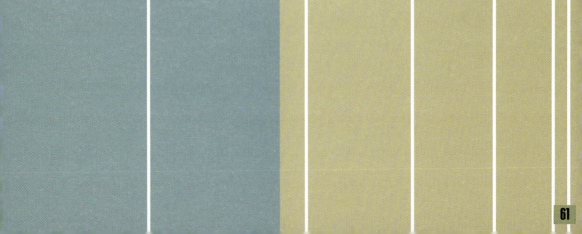

Chapter Seven: Tired of the Freak Show Creating a New You

Next time you're in the school cafeteria or at a youth group meeting, try a little experiment. Look around you. That's right—allow your eyes to take a long, slow pan across the room. So, what do you see? Cliques. Herds of guys and girls who never seem to cross an invisible line that separates the classes.

The cool kids (usually the jocks and prom queens, right?) claim one part of the room. The skaters, surfers, and metal heads hang out in another. The science and computer kids try to lie low somewhere in a corner. How about YOU? Where do you fit into the picture? Do you feel like you're part of the middle mass of nothingness, someone who just blends into the tabletops? Or do you feel as if every eye is on YOU—like you're the featured act in today's teenage freak show?

Guess what? You're NOT a freak—or a zero. And despite what herd you run with, your life counts. So keep reading, because on the pages that follow, we'll zero in on what's truly cool . . . and what's not. We'll help you deal with bullies, and we'll even give you a can't-lose strategy for building confidence and a better new you.

The Cruel "Cool Code"

It's an unfair rule among many teenage guys: If you don't look, talk, or act a certain way—if you don't fall into the right category—you end up a target for bullying and teasing.

Take 15-year-old David, for example. This northern California kid is a talented artist who dreams about one day becoming president of his own comic book company—or maybe even filling an upscale New York art gallery with his masterpieces. Yet he feels as if every other guy at his school cares about only one thing: scoring at the next party. Despite being excited about his future and all the possibilities God has set before him, he can't help noticing that too many other boys his age put on cynical acts, making everyone think that nothing but the moment really matters.

"Here's the crazy thing," David says. "I catch myself wondering if something is wrong with *me*. Some guys call me 'geek' or 'church boy.' It really hurts. Why do teens have to act so cruel?"

answer: too many guys are trapped in a lie . . .

. . . the lie that they're worthless unless they hang with the popular crowd.

. . . the lie that cool = having a muscle-bound body, possessing Herculean strength, and strutting through the mall with the absolute most drop-dead beautiful, super-model-cheerleader-type babe glued to your arm.

. . . the lie that measuring up as a man means living up to an impossible "cool code": always being a tough guy, never showing weakness, and—above all—never expressing your true feelings.

popularity: a losing game?

Hand in hand with the cool code is the popularity game.

Playing the popularity game means doing what's socially acceptable. Though the rules are different in each part of the world, here are a few of the most familiar ones: wear the right clothes, go to the right parties, use the right language (which usually means swearing), and keep God at just the right distance (at least in public).

Social survival for many guys—even those who claim to be Christians—is dependent upon how they measure up in these areas. If they don't measure up, they're not cool. And if they're not cool, what are they?

Wannabes! So guys like you spend every waking moment trying to break into the cool crowd. But what happens if they can't break in? They end up feeling pretty bad about themselves. They even begin thinking that they're outcasts, convinced that they'll never be accepted.

the price of popularity

Face it, we all want to fit in. It's why we wear low-riding, leg-flaring baggies one year, then switch to acid-washed, plaid wrestling singlets the next. (Okay, let's pray that those will never be in style.) It's also why we just *have* to have the latest CD from DJ Wack or 186 Degrees.

It's all about acceptance. Unfortunately, too many guys are willing to go too far to try to be popular. Of course, there ARE exceptions to this cruel game. There are confident Christian guys who aren't caught up in what others think—young men who are clued in to the *right* definition of cool.

COOL REDEFINED

Tired of the rigid cool code? Sick of playing the popularity game? Then it's time for a change. It's time to let the One who created you and everything in this world, not the so-called popular people, navigate your life. It's time to let the God of all eternity, not a passing crowd, define what is and isn't cool. How?

Learn what God really thinks of you. We've all heard that God loves us. And we know that God allowed His Son, Jesus Christ, to die on a cross and pay the penalty of our sin—which demonstrates the extent of His love. Then why don't we act as if this is the most incredible news we've ever heard? If God—the One who created us—says we are worthy of *His* love, why do we pursue what our culture thinks is cool in order to feel good about ourselves?

Understand that you were made for much more than parties and popularity. In fact, the Lord doesn't measure your worth the way people do. The Bible says He sets little value on the things we treasure so much, especially the three B's: brains, outer beauty, and bucks. Why? Because these diversions often mess up our self-confidence and get in the way of our knowing Christ deeper and fulfilling His will for our lives.

Strive for GREATNESS. Here are some keys: Know Jesus personally, saturate your mind with Scripture, pray, rely on God's strength when you're weak, and seek the kind of joy that can only come from a hope in heaven, not from the things of this world. (Crack open your Bible and read Colossians 1:9-23 for more ideas.) Bottom line: Value what Jesus values. He will guide you along a path that leads to purpose and meaning in life—that is, if you let Him.

confidence clues

clue no. 1: take inventory

Sometime soon, stand in front of a full-length mirror and evaluate the person you see. As you study the kid in the mirror, ask yourself some honest questions: *Who am I? Is this the best me? Is there room for improvement? What can I change? What must I accept about myself?*

Next, vow to God and to yourself to make the most out of what you have. Seek to improve the things that are within your power to change, and accept what you cannot change.

Ask the Lord to help you make up for your weaknesses by concentrating on your strengths. In other words, if you're not exactly crazy about your looks, tell yourself this: *So I'm not male model material. Big deal—I'm not alone! Besides, my self-worth isn't dependent on the arrangement of my body. I'll put my energy into a skill that'll help me feel good about myself. I'm a talented _____* (insert the word that applies to you, such as musician, artist, athlete). *I'll continue to improve this skill and become the best I can be.*

clue no. 2: focus on the right image—christ's

As you stand in front of the mirror, think about all the other times you've spent in that very spot, flexing your muscles, combing your hair, checking out those new clothes—expending so much effort seeking acceptance. Now consider this: Christ "had no beauty or majesty to attract us to him, nothing in his appearance that we should desire him" (Isaiah 53:2). People were attracted to Jesus because His beauty was internal. His heart emanated unlimited love. The peace in His eyes drew crowds. The joy of His smile was contagious. Seek to make His focus your own.

clue no. 3: get an attitude adjustment

Proverbs 15:4 says:

> The tongue that brings healing is a tree of life,
> but a deceitful tongue crushes the spirit.

Begin to replace "I don't know how" with "Now is the time for me to learn." Replace "I can't" with "I will."

Keep in mind that it's not where you are at that's important; it's where you're headed. Take Michael Jordan, for example. He got cut from a basketball team during his early years. When that happened, the rejection was probably quite painful for him. Yet he didn't remain discouraged for long, and he didn't give up.

clue no. 4: beware of the company you keep

Proverbs 13:20 says:

> He who walks with the wise grows wise,
> but a companion of fools suffers harm.

In other words, a friend of winners will be a winner but a friend of fools will die. Now check out 1 Corinthians 15:33-34: "Do not be misled: 'Bad company corrupts good character.' Come back to your senses as you ought, and stop sinning; for there are some who are ignorant of God—I say this to your shame."

FRIENDSHIP: ASSEMBLY REQUIRED!

■ Tell others the truth about who they are. Be one of the few who remind their friends of their strengths and abilities.

■ Cut back on the cuts! Don't let a few "friendly" put-downs become a habit. Vow to be different.

■ Defend your friends, especially when someone is talking bad behind their backs. Also, never give in to the gossip game.

■ Point others to the One who will always tell them the truth.

Endless teasing. Constant humiliation. Fifteen-year-old Andy was at his breaking point. He lay on the ground by a basketball court, buckled like a crumpled, discarded Pepsi can.

"You're an absolute loser," taunted one of the boys who hit him.

"Don't even think about shooting hoops with us," shouted another. "We're way out of your league, dweeb."

Suddenly, a whistle blew, and the boys scattered, leaving Andy alone.

"What's this all about, son?" barked the school's coach.

Andy raised his head and tried to blink away the tears. "They hate me," he mumbled. "Everybody hates me 'cause I'm skinny and clumsy . . . and not a jock."

"Look, sports just isn't your thing," the coach responded, helping Andy to his feet. "Don't sweat the teasing. Just be a man, tough it out, and keep going."

Andy's head began to swim. *If this is manhood, then I don't want it. Something MUST change!*

ENOUGH IS ENOUGH!

Like countless other guys his age, Andy managed to survive his teen years—but not without a few nasty scars.

"The constant teasing literally ripped apart my confidence," says Andy, who is now in his early twenties. "Yet all I heard from coaches, teachers, and parents was the same thing: 'Just ignore it. Teasing is a part of being a guy.' I felt trapped and alone. I desperately needed help, but I didn't know where to turn."

UNPLUGGING THE PAIN

Does this sound familiar? The hostile teen world you must endure hasn't changed much from Andy's day. Teasing and bullying is still a way of life among your peers, not to mention a way to survive. Regardless of the cool person you are on the inside, if you appear slightly different from the crowd, you risk getting the walls of your brain sprayed with all kinds of ugly graffiti—words like *WIMP, LOSER, NERD!*

Maybe you're a victim. Or maybe you think that you have to hurt others in order to avoid being a target. Regardless, like so many other guys, you probably think that the only answer is to shut up and fit in at any cost rather than to care or understand. Yet, as Andy so wisely put it, "Something must change."

WHAT YOU CAN DO

Build a "shield of friends." Find at least one or two other guys your age who will be true, unconditional friends. Also, surround yourself with like-minded peers and adults who will stand by your side when a bully tries to strike.

Talk it out. Tell your parents, a youth leader, or a school counselor what's going on. Be honest with them about your anger and frustration. Above all, don't keep it in; that's not fair to you.

Learn to value your value. Whenever word bullets and brain graffiti begin to mess with your mind, stop and remind yourself of two awesome truths:

1. You were created by God Almighty, the God of the universe, and if God is for you, who can be against you? (See Romans 8:31.)

2. You can do all things through Christ, who gives you strength. (See Philippians 4:13.)

Know the truth. People who put you down are only trying to deal with their own lousy self-image. It's like they're thinking, *If I can't bring myself up any higher, maybe I can bring someone else down.*

Don't become a bully. Some guys who are teased turn into bullies themselves. Don't do it. Remember, hate begets hate. Besides, you'd end up slicing up someone else's self-esteem, which only continues the ugly cycle. Instead, be the one who builds others up.

Get some "godly" guidance. Consider this: During His time on earth, Jesus Christ was hit with more hateful graffiti than any human could ever bear (see 1 Peter 2:21-23). He, more than anyone else, understands. He'll help you through this.

a word to bullies

As a Christian young man, it's up to you to promote change. How? Consider this.

If you're a bully, even if you think it's just in fun—knock it off! Never dismiss it as harmless boyhood behavior or as a "hardening experience" that will prepare you and your friends for manhood.

Stand up for the underdog. What should you do if you see some guy being picked on? Check out what God has to say about this: "He will defend the afflicted among the people" (Psalm 72:4). "Defend the cause of the weak" (Psalm 82:3). Sounds pretty clear-cut. If possible, step in and let the bully know that what he's doing is harmful.

But be careful. If there's a chance of violence when you intervene, go first to a teacher or the principal. It's not snitching; it's helping a classmate. It also shows real courage.

Create a safe harbor where you and your friends can retreat. Let your bullied friend know that you take his dilemma seriously and that you care. Use your gifts for others. Use your size not to pick on others but to fight for those who can't fight for themselves.

art three: Waiting, Dating, Relating

CHAPTER EIGHT: SEX—WHAT IT IS, WHAT IS ISN'T ▌▌▌ ▌ ▌ ▌▌▌ ▌▌ ▌

Sex is everywhere.

You're kicking back with the TV remote. Click. Nudity. Click. Full-blown sex scene. Even the commercials are serving up half-naked women.

You're surfing the Web for school research. All of a sudden you're bombarded with suggestive ads and sleazy sites blatantly inviting you to sex, sex, sex. Yikes!

You head to the superplex to check out the latest flick. Less than 10 minutes into the movie, the love theme plays and the stars take a tumble. Man, they're not leaving much to the imagination.

You grab one of Chanelle's girl mags on a 14-hour missions trip bus ride. Whoa! This is supposed to be the fashion issue, but these models are hardly wearing anything. And what's up with all the explicit Q & A columns?

You're pumped on the way home from youth group and really feeling focused on God. You glance out the car window. BAM! A 30-foot temptress in a skimpy bikini suggestively stares at you from a billboard.

There's no way around it. We live in a sexualized society. Businesses use sex to sell everything. Musicians sing about it. Many schools teach that everything is fine as long as you wear a condom. It's a tough time to be a guy who's trying to stay pure, but you can make it. There's hope!

GOOD SEX—GOD'S WAY ▌ ▌▌▌ ▌▌ ▌

Do you think about sex? Do you want sex? Do you want to please God?

No, these aren't trick questions. It's okay, you can admit it. All of us guys think about sex, and your teens years are the time when your body shifts into the high gear of sexual development. (For more on that, check out chapter four.)

But you said "sex" and "God" in the same paragraph! Exactly. Maybe you haven't heard much about sex in your church. That's unfortunate. Sex can be an awkward topic to talk about, but it's one that every Christian deals with. Why? Because every Christian is human.

God created sex. *Yeah, I know; He created everything.* Well, have you ever *really* thought about that? God created sex. He chose to make it. It wasn't an afterthought or something bad that entered the world with sin.

God looked at this Adam He'd just created and realized that he needed a partner. So He created one:

THOU SHALT

woman. And what did God tell them to do? "Be fruitful and multiply." How? S-e-x.

Genesis 1:31 says, "God saw all that he had made, and it was very good." Not just good—*very* good. And that includes sex.

what is sex?

Sex is connection, communication, and union on the deepest possible human level. Sex is two people joining together in a way that makes them one. It's physical and more. Sex is also emotional, mental, and spiritual. It is ultimate trust and vulnerability. Sex is creation; it has the power to form new life. Sex is the expression of love and the celebration of commitment. It can be fun, thrilling, passionate, and deep when used right. It can be unsatisfying, painful, cruel, and dangerous when misused.

WHY ALL THE RULES?

Sex is like fire. In the right place—like a fireplace or a fire pit—fire can save your life by warming you up. In the wrong place—like your house or a forest—fire can kill you. That's why God set up guidelines for sex. Was He trying to take away all the fun? No, He knew that this was a very powerful gift, one with the power to connect—or destroy—two people on the deepest level. That's why He made it a gift to be shared between one man and one woman within the bonds of marriage.

Of course, along with every other good thing he could get his hands on, Satan twisted and perverted sex.

Talk about damage and destruction: addiction, disease, rape, incest, exploitation, even death. There's plenty of the dark side.

The trick is to stay focused on God's plan and timing and to glorify Him with your sex. Sound strange? It's not. God is pleased when two of His children celebrate their love and marriage commitment with sex. Yeah, you think, *I'd love to do that, but I've got a long way to go till marriage and no clue about who my wife will be.* True, but you can still glorify God with your sexuality. In fact, you can worship God with it.

How? By letting Him have control of your sexuality and following His path of purity while you wait. Romans 12:1 calls it "offer[ing] your bodies as living sacrifices, holy and pleasing to God." It's laying those sexual feelings and desires on God's altar and trusting Him to protect them until His time.

COMANDMENTS

1
2
3
4
5
6
7
8
9
10

WHAT THE BIBLE SAYS ABOUT SEX

Check out:

Genesis 2:21-25	1 Corinthians 7:1-11
Job 31:1	Galatians 5:19
Proverbs 5	Ephesians 5:3
Proverbs 6:27-29	Colossians 3:1-10
Proverbs 7	1 Thessalonians 4:3-7
Song of Solomon 2:7	Titus 2:12-13
Matthew 5:27-30	Hebrews 13:4
1 Corinthians 6:12-20	Revelation 21:8

BLASTING THE MYTHS

Lies about sex are everywhere, especially in the media. Some are easy to recognize. Others are sneakily subtle. Do any of these sound familiar?

WHAT HOLLYWOOD SAYS:

- Everybody's doing it.
- Having sex makes you a man.
- Sex proves love.
- You can't control it; just do it.
- Sex is a game; score as much as you can.
- You can keep it casual.
- Just wait till you're ready—then everything's fine.
- A condom will keep you safe.
- Teens *will* have sex; nothing can stop them.
- When she says no, she really means yes.
- Sex always works perfectly and romantically, complete with a love-theme soundtrack.
- Youth is the time for good, wild sex.
- *Virginity* is a bad word.

WHAT GOD SAYS:

Every lie is a distortion of the truth. Here are some truths about sex.

- Not everybody's doing it.
- A real man is able to control his body and sexual urges.
- Real love wants God's best for another.
- Passion is strong, but God's strength is stronger.
- No one has ever died from lack of sex.
- Sex is an expression of love. The loser is the one who grows callous to intimate commitment.
- Casual sex always leaves a mark, emotionally if not physically.
- Sex is about God's timetable—marriage—not your feelings.
- Condoms aren't guaranteed to stop all sexually transmitted diseases, and they're worthless against emotional scars.
- Teens are capable of sexual control; they're not animals.
- No means no. A guy never has a right to a girl's body against her wishes.
- Sex takes communication and trust. It rarely looks just like movie love scenes.
- A University of Chicago study found that those most consistently satisfied sexually were—surprise!—married couples.
- Once virginity is gone, you can never get it back. Anyone can have sex. Not everyone can be a virgin.

LOVE **VERSUS LUST** ▐ ▌ ▌ ▌ ▌ ▌ ▌ ▐

Lust is a beast—a sharp-fanged, beady-eyed, crooked-clawed, drooling monster of a beast. It can sink its venom into any area of desire to poison with its self-centered craving, but it especially loves sex. And it is never satisfied.

Lust hates love. The two are archenemies, polar opposites. But lust is a master of deception. Its favorite disguise? Love.

"My Bible study of 10 guys recognized what an obstacle wandering eyes are to our faith. So we decided that anytime we looked at a girl with the least bit of lust, we must do 10 push-ups on the spot. I even did a set of 10 in the huddle during a football game after catching myself staring at the opposing team's manager.

"The cure for the disease of lust is primarily to keep your eyes up, focused on the Lord. Girls definitely do not deserve to be looked upon as objects of lust. Rather, they are unique, beautiful creatures of God."

—Tony Ariniello, 17, Boulder, Colorado

LUST SAYS:

- Me, me, me.
- Now.
- More—more.
- If it feels good, do it.
- Give it to me.
- I can't wait.

LOVE SAYS:

- You
- Later—when it's right.
- Less. Let's steer clear of temptation.
- I'll put your future before my short-term pleasure.
- I'll do what it takes to protect your purity.
- I'm willing to wait.

MIND CONTROL, THOUGHT PATROL

Quiz: What's the most important male sex organ?

Nope, not that one. It's the one between your ears: your brain. Sexual arousal starts in the mind—sometimes subconsciously—and the nervous system triggers your body to respond, complete with increased heart rate and erect penis.

That means the key to counterattacking lust is to filter what you take into your brain. What connects your brain to the rest of the world? Your senses. And for guys, probably the most important sexual sense is sight. It's the way God wired us: We're turned on visually.

Why do you think porn is such a huge industry and such a stumbling block even to committed Christian guys? One little glance, one quick peek and—*wham*—sex on the brain.

So, what's a guy to do? Here are a few tips for heading off lust:

- Be like a Boy Scout—always prepared. There are two types of turn-on tempters: the ones you can avoid and the ones you can't. You can't do anything about the girl passing you on the street, but you can avoid the Playboy Channel on TV. Know that temptation is always just around the corner. Keep your guard up.

- Steer clear of known fantasy feeders: provocative movies, songs, magazines, Web sites. You've got enough sexual urges without stirring up more on purpose.

- Stay busy. King David was kicking back on the palace roof instead of being in battle with his men when he took his sexual fall (2 Samuel 11). Lounging all the time is an open invitation to fill the boredom with lust.

- Watch who you hang with. Your friends' language, habits, attitudes, and humor will impact you.

- Arm your brain with Scripture. Memorize a few verses related to sexual purity. When temptation strikes, say them out loud. There's power in God's Word.

IT'LL GO AWAY ONCE I GET MARRIED

If only I can just get married, then my beautiful, hot, sexy wife, who totally loves the Lord, can fulfill all my sexual fantasies. I won't have to struggle with lust anymore.

Have you ever found yourself thinking that? You're pretty normal if you have. You're also wrong—in a couple of ways.

1. Marriage is fantastic, and sex is wonderful to share with your wife. But neither being married nor having sex regularly has the magical power to instantly change you into something you're not.

You mean I'm stuck with this struggle for the rest of my life?

Maybe. God can change your heart, and you can learn to guard your heart and mind better. But marriage just means you have a partner to share your life with: the good, the bad, and the struggles. And having sex doesn't make you immune to lust.

They're enemies, remember? Why should lust quit attacking when you've found the deepest love of your life? Instead, it will just switch tactics and start trying to convince you that the other guy's woman is more attractive than yours.

2. It's great to have high standards for your future wife, but where are your expectations coming from? Are you thinking about godly character or airbrushed swimsuit-model images? Sure, you want to be physically attracted to your wife, but how would you like it if she compared you with every studly action-movie hero? Not quite fair, is it?

You can pollute or purify your mind. Your future wife will thank you for choosing the latter. And you'll thank yourself for building habits that will carry you through the marathon of beating lust.

CHAPTER NINE: WAITING ISN'T WEIRD

Ever feel like you're the only one who's waiting, or trying to follow God's plan for sex? Sometimes it can seem awfully lonely sticking to your virginity. In most areas of morality it's harder to do what's right than to do what's wrong; the same is true for sex.

But you're not alone. As long as there has been a "safe sex" agenda saying, "Just use protection, and everything's okay," there has also been a moral revolution of teens who are willing—and committed—to wait. Not just a few, but hundreds of thousands, even millions.

In fact, more are saying no than yes to premarital sex. During the 1990s, the percentage of teens who had intercourse dropped from 54 percent to 49 percent, according to data from the Centers for Disease Control and Prevention. That's a majority of virgins!

HOW FAR IS TOO FAR?

It's the question everybody wants answered. But it's coming from the wrong angle.

If a land mine lay in a field with a trigger wire stretched tight nearby, would you push it to see how close you could come without setting off the explosive? Only if you had a death wish. You'd stay as far away as possible from that bomb, the trigger, and even the field.

Sexual purity isn't about finding the line and then seeing how close you can come to it without stepping over. It's about maintaining your sexual innocence and waiting for marriage and sex in God's time.

guy talk

"My virginity is a gift I want to give my future wife. You can only give it once."

—Alex Fitzgerald, 18
Burlington, North Carolina

"Sex is something made especially for marriage. To go around having it with any girl would show you don't have much consideration for God's gift."

—Roland Wiley, 19
Altadena, California

"I want to show guys my age that you don't have to go out and have sex to be a man ... or to be cool."

—Rob Ladd
Nashville, Tennessee

God didn't do eeny-meeny-miney-mo to decide on His standards and guidelines for sex. Remember? He made sex, so He understands it better than anyone, both its powers and its dangers. He also knows the benefits of saving sex for your wife. Here are a few reasons that make waiting worth it.

No diseases. Can you imagine having to tell your future wife that you have HIV, herpes, gonorrhea, syphilis, genital warts, human papillomavirus, or another destructive STD? Worse, can you imagine finding out that you've given your wife a potentially deadly disease that you didn't even know you had? How about having your life cut short from AIDS before you even get married? A few minutes of pleasure aren't worth a lifetime of suffering.

No fatherhood. Are you ready to be a dad? *Who, me? I'm still just a kid myself!* It only takes once to get someone pregnant—and to change your life forever. Real life responsibility will hit hard and fast. Will you marry the mother? How will you financially support yourself and your baby? How will you raise the child? There's always abortion; it's an easy out, right? Wrong! It may physically free you from the responsibilities of parenthood, but you'll deal with the guilt and emotional scars—perhaps for your whole life—of knowing that you killed your own child.

No sexual baggage. Picture this: It's your wedding night. You've eaten the cake and taken the pictures and finally it's just you and your wife in the secluded bridal suite of a fancy hotel. *Woo-hoo!* You thought this part would never come: no more saying no; everything is totally okay; God says go for it. You begin kissing your new bride, but wait! What's going on? There's that girl from spring break . . . and your old girlfriend . . . and—wait a minute!—you know that other girl, too! What?! The whole room is filled with your past sexual partners!

Okay, so they won't really be there physically, but they will be there emotionally. Sex, even if it's supposed to be "casual," has the mysterious power of connecting people and making them one—the Bible calls it "one flesh" (Genesis 2:24). Can God bring forgiveness and healing? Absolutely. But the memories or comparisons and the fact that you connected to that other girl in such an intimate way will have to be dealt with between you and your wife and will always remain.

No scars. That one-flesh thing? It means that sex is the ultimate superglue between people. You can pull away, but something's gonna tear. Some of that "one flesh" you've created is going to tear away from you forever. Maybe you won't even feel it at first, but eventually the wounds will fester before they heal. You'll see the scars.

No guilt. Guilt can be a killer. Make no mistake, God can and does forgive the worst sins, including sexual sins. But often we have a hard time forgiving ourselves. To make it worse, Satan loves to take every opportunity to fling our sins in our face, telling us that we're guilty and condemned. You can get past that kind of pain, but why put yourself in the position in the first place?

Fun freedom. Waiting for sex until your honeymoon will build the foundation for a lifetime of guilt-free, comparison-free, disease-free, fully connected and committed sexual satisfaction. Don't you think that's worth waiting for?

making a pact for purity

Don't just sit there waiting to try to say no to sexual temptation. Now is the time to take present and future temptation head-on, make your stand, and pursue purity. Here's how:

Act with accountability. There's strength in numbers, and all you need is a buddy or two to share your commitment.

Pray for your accountability partners. And pray with them for God's strength.

Take a dare on your dad. Psyche yourself up to talk honestly with your dad about your sexual struggles. He can give you wisdom, suggestions, and even more accountability. If your dad's not in the picture, find a relative, pastor, youth leader, or even one of your friend's dads.

Stand strong. Get a purity cross, necklace, or ring that you can wear all the time to remind you of your commitment.

Purge any porn. Do the same with any other sexual material that causes you to fall.

Find freedom through forgiveness. If you've already made mistakes, read 1 John 1:9 and Psalm 103:11-12. The all-powerful God forgives you; how can tiny you hold your sin against you? Accept His forgiveness and healing, let go of the past, and move on in purity.

Move on with a new mind. God wants to renew your mind and shape your thinking about sex. Read His Word, memorize Scripture to keep you on track, and check out some of the resources listed at the end of this chapter. Also avoid any TV programs, movies, music, Web sites, jokes, or friends who give you warped messages about sex.

Beef up your boundaries. Determine now how far is too far on the path of purity. Don't just ask, "Is it wrong?" Rather, ask, "Is it wise or good for me?" Make your limits clear to your accountability partners and have them hold you to 'em.

I've already gone too far

So you messed up? Crossed the line? Went too far? Sinned?

Maybe it was porn. Maybe it was lust—letting that fantasy life run way out of line. Maybe things got out of control with that girl. Maybe you went all the way. Maybe it was once. Maybe it's become a pattern, a habit, an addiction.

Yeah, well, we have two things to say to you, mister. You're not alone, and God knows.

What? You're not gonna tell me I'm wrong, beat me up, blast and condemn me?

No way. Satan has already done too much of that and told you there's more if you dare let anybody know about your deepest, darkest sins. It's just another one of his lies.

Look at those two things again.

You're not alone. There are far too many casualties on the road to sexual purity. There are many causes, but the silence of the sexual struggle has pushed too many Christian guys over the edge. You're not alone in your struggle. You're not alone in your failure. And you don't have to be alone in your healing.

God knows. You've tried to hide it long enough. Maybe you confessed it to Him, but you're still dealing with guilt, flogging yourself for your failure, thinking God won't notice. Maybe you're still hoping He was looking the other way that night you . . .

He knows. That's not a bad thing; it's the best possible thing. Get it? God knows your deepest secrets and sins—and He loves you anyway! If you have a personal relationship with Him, you're not condemned for what you did. God doesn't hold it against you. Jesus died on the cross for that exact failure. When you confessed it to Him, He threw it as far away as the east is from the west. That's not just California to New York; that's way out beyond the edges of the universe. It's gone.

SHAKE OFF THE SHAME

Shame is guilt run out of control. It's what the devil uses to tell you that, because of whatever you did, you are bad, worthless, beyond God's love or forgiveness. Those *feelings* can be real, but the *fact* is that it's another lie.

No matter what you've done, how many times, with whom, or where, there's hope and forgiveness in Jesus. He wants you to experience both. He wants to restore your purity. And He can do it.

There may be some pain or tough consequences to work through, but Jesus wants to carry you through them. Give up your guilt and shame to Him and let Him have control of your sexuality. Turn to page 86 and make a pact for purity.

If you've crossed too many lines with another person, you may also need to seek her forgiveness. This can be difficult, but it can also be a big step toward healing.

When it comes to future relationships, you may need to abstain from all physical affection. It's tough to go backward, especially if you've been all the way. But tough times call for tough measures. It will be worth it when your wedding night is a celebration of all that God has done to restore your sexual purity.

HELPFUL resources

BOOKS

No Apologies: The Truth About Life, Love, & Sex
(Focus on the Family/Tyndale House)

Pure Excitement by Joe White
(Focus on the Family/Tyndale House)

What Hollywood Won't Tell You About Sex, Love, and Dating by Greg Johnson and Susie Shellenberger
(Regal Books)

Who Moved the Goalposts? by Bob and Dana Gresh
(Moody Press)

TAPES

A Message to Teens About Sex by Fran Sciacca

Dr. Dobson on Teens and Sex by Dr. James Dobson

True Love Waits by Dr. Richard Ross, Amy Stephens, and Dr. James Dobson

Clean Heart for a New Start: Restoring Spiritual Virginity by Josh McDowell

VIDEOS

No Apologies: The Truth About Life, Love, & Sex by Focus on the Family

The Myth of Safe Sex by Dr. James Dobson

BOOKLETS

"A Crime of Force: The Horrifying Reality of Sexual Abuse" by Focus on the Family

"Hold On to Your Heart: Making the Most of the Gift God Gave You" by Amy Stephens

"In Your Face . . . In Your Mind: Resisting the Power of Pornography" by Steve Watters

WEB SITES

True Love Waits (www.truelovewaits.com)
Abstinence Clearinghouse (www.abstinence.net)

You can order any of these resources by calling
(800) A-FAMILY (232-6459) or by visiting www.family.org.

CHAPTER TEN

BOY MEETS GIRL ▌▌ ▌ ▌▌▌▌▌ ▌▌ ▌

Quick—what are you thinking about? C'mon, be honest. Besides nothin', we know you've got girls on your mind. Breakaway gets letters all the time asking questions about how to tell if Leanne really likes you, or how to handle it because Janelle broke up with you, or . . . You get the picture.

Hey, it's only natural. You probably remember the day not so long ago when those gross, cootie-infested giiiirls started looking good and seeming awfully interesting. Of course, when it comes to females, "interesting" includes a whole lot of confusing.

get a clue about your g.q. (girl quotient) ▌ ▌▌▌ ▌▌ ▌ ▌

Do you know your G.Q.? Just like your I.Q. (Intelligence Quotient) is supposed to tell how smart you are, your G.Q. lets you know how smart you are when it comes to understanding, treating, and relating to girls. It's your Girl Intelligence Quotient. Never heard of it? Neither had we until we made it up. But it's time to find out what yours is: Just take your best shot at the questions scattered throughout this chapter. Don't worry, you'll find plenty of tips to raise your G.Q. a few points.

every damsel's different

Girls are complex creatures, so we won't claim that these wise insights apply to every girl out there. Just like you have your own personality and preferences, so does every female. The good thing is that they're putting just as much energy into trying to understand you. Our tips will give you some insight into the minds of girls worth getting to know a little better.

? QUIZ Q 1

Mariah's a great friend. You've hung out a lot. You even talk on the phone sometimes. So the other day at Taco Bell she starts asking if you think all these girls in the restaurant are good-looking. Okay, whatever. But then she says, "Do you think I'm pretty?" After you choke on your chalupa, you . . .

A totally ignore her question and keep shouting "Ohhh, la chica!" every time a girl walks by.

B answer, "Umm, well, you're . . . okay. Are you gonna eat the rest of that taco grande?"

C tell her, "Yeah, but it's really cool that you're not totally into your looks or worrying about your image all the time."

QUIZ Q 2

You've been reading "What Girls Think" in your favorite mag, and all these babes keep talking about sensitive guys. You decide to give it a try. If chicks dig sensitive, then you'll show Sarah that you're the Mac-Daddy of sensitivity. So you . . .

A pinch yourself until the tears are flowing freely, then run up, hug Sarah, and tell her between sobs how special she is to you.

B invite her over to watch *Bambi* and give her a cute little stuffed deer to hold while she cries.

C talk to her about life and listen closely when she tells you what she's struggling with. You send a note to encourage her and let her know you're praying for her.

aliens among us ▌▌▌▌▌ ▌▌ ▌ ▌

Girls might as well be aliens, right? I mean, they talk different—or at least more. They *act* different— what's with all the hugging and crying? They *think* different—c'mon, what's not to admire about the human body's amazing ability to make so many funky sounds, both real and imitated? They *smell* different—well, the flowery aroma does beat your best friend's dirty-gym-sock scent covered with Pine Forest Speed Stick. They even *look* different—okay, this one you're really glad about.

It's like they came from some other planet. Maybe there's even some obscure Old Testament verse that talks about God directing the mother ship in from outer space and landing it in the Garden of Eden. Uh, sorry—but no.

Sure, there are similarities. But God did create men and women differently and made them to complement each other. No, not "compliment," which is to say nice things to each other (although that is a good idea). We mean that men and women are to use their strengths to help the other's weaknesses.

GIRL TALK

"Girls and guys are completely different. Half the time we don't know what we want. So the best thing is just to be there for a girl when she needs to talk or have a shoulder to cry on."

—Becky Pulaski, 16
Brownwood, Texas

"I don't know if anyone will truly understand a woman's emotions, but, guys, we need a lot of encouragement."

—Emily Oswell, 15
Bellevue, Washington

"Be patient and talk to us. Most of the time we'll tell you what's going on inside if we think you care."

—Linnea Shannon, 17
Oroville, Washington

clue no. one

Girls get slammed from every side with unrealistic pressures from TV, advertisements, movies, and magazines telling them they've got to look just right to receive any attention or get anywhere in this society. Yeah, it's true for guys, too. But one look at a magazine rack will tell you that girls get that times 10. We all need to feel valued, and it's especially important to girls to know that they're attractive. Take 2 bonus points if you picked **C.** Not only did you validate her outer looks, but you also encouraged her for focusing on inner beauty—something the Bible says is more important for anyone. (Check out 1 Samuel 16:7 and 1 Peter 3:3-4.)

talking to girls | | | | | | | | | |

You've been staring at her all during lunch period for the past two weeks. You're pretty sure she's caught you looking at her a few times. But every time you try to get up the nerve to talk, your stomach does a near-perfect simulation of the quadruple-loop Super Pukifier, and your mouth would *swear* you just swallowed all the sand in Egypt.

Yeah, talking to girls can be nerve-racking. But here are some tips to help tame the butterflies.

Be yourself. Most girls will see right through an act eventually if not immediately. Talk about the things that you like to do, that you are interested in, and that are real in your life. Leave the cheesy lines at home.

Find something in common. Got a class together? You're both left-handed? You were both at the Audio Adrenaline concert last summer? Shared experiences or interests will get the words flowing much more comfortably.

Ask questions. This is especially good for you shy guys. Throw out one sentence, then sit back and listen for four paragraphs. Not only do questions show you're interested in the other person, but also the answers help you get to know the girl. Avoid yes-or-no questions. Instead of "Do you like school?" try "What's your favorite class, and why?" Hint: "Why" is always a great conversation booster.

Listen to the answers. Sure, you're nervous, but concentrating so hard on your next question that you don't hear a word she says gets you nowhere. Remember, girls are into all this communication stuff, so they can tell when you're zoning out.

Jotting down a list ahead of time is a good idea—think of it as your game plan. But once you're live in the game, use the plan as your backup. The conversation should be like a good game of catch: You throw her a question; she tosses an answer back. Then she lobs you a question of her own. Get the idea? It's no good, though, if one person holds on to the ball—or the talking—for too long.

Relax. Keep your eyes on the big picture. Believe it or not, there are more important things in life than girls—for example, your faith and what God is doing in your life. So your conversation flops? God is still in control of your love life. Chalk it up to conversation practice and ask God what He wants to teach you. Maybe you'll have another chance to talk to her; maybe you'll remember what not to say 10 years from now when you're talking to your eventual wife for the first time.

guy talk

"When it comes to talking with girls, I've made a lot of mistakes. I've acted like anybody but myself. I soon learned that if a girl ended up liking me, she'd be attracted to the person I was pretending to be, not the REAL me. Now that I've made an effort to be myself, I think girls feel more comfortable talking to me, too."

—J.Y.
Radnor, Ohio

clue no. two

Women want to know what's going on inside. You know, what you're thinking and feeling. Their emotions are usually closer to the surface; that's why they might cry more often for a friend or in a sad movie or when someone throws a put-down their way. It's also why they like to talk about what he said and she said and what it really means that he really likes her but she's not sure and . . .

That doesn't mean they want a guy to be just like them. "Opposites attract" is often true. That's why extra-emotional girls are often attracted to the strong, silent type. But even then, they spend most of the time asking Mr. Silent what he's thinking and feeling. They don't want a guy who's a blubbering puddle of tears. But they love it when a guy shows compassion for others, cares enough to listen, and shares what he's thinking and feeling.

Every time you get within 50 yards of Hayley, your knees shake and your stomach thinks it's on a trampoline. She's kind, funny, beautiful—and a Christian! *It's time she notices me,* you decide. So you . . .

A punch her in the shoulder, pull her hair, and knock her books out of her hands, especially when all your friends are around to laugh.

B tattoo her name across your back and run through the halls waving a flag that says, "Hayley, I love you!"

C take a deep breath, go to her locker, and say hi. Walk her to class and ask questions that help you get to know her a little better.

Ever since you've both been going to that Bible study on Wednesday nights, you've been thinking, *Gabriela's so easy to talk to. I might be starting to like her.* But then at school she comes over to talk to you while you're with the guys—right in the middle of your daily lunchtime burping contest! You . . .

A take a big gulp of air and in one rippin' belch say, "Hey, no chicks allowed!" You can't let the guys know you like a girl!

B grunt and nod to acknowledge her presence, then disappear into the guy's bathroom as quickly as you can.

C smile and say, "Hi . . . and, uh, excuse me." Ask your friends to cut it out while she's around, introduce them all, and invite her to sit down.

girl talk

"I look for a guy who is considerate of other people's feelings and who acts like a gentleman by doing things such as opening the door for me. It's also important that a guy act the same around his other friends as he does around me."

—Becky Staple, 17
Apache Junction, Arizona

clue no. three

We guys lose as much sweat trying to get up the nerve to talk to that cute girl in fourth period as we do in a week's worth of soccer practices. Hey, girls get a little nervous too, but they tell us all the time, "We just want guys to talk to us." Trust us, just be yourself and use a few words to find out who Hayley really is. It'll open the door to friendship and tame those monster butterflies.

clue no. four

Girls want guys to be real and treat them the same no matter who's around. But you can't have the guys rag on you about a girl, right? Wrong. So you may feel a little embarrassed 'cause you secretly like her a little. But if Gabriela's really such a cool friend, then you'll be a cool friend right back to her. Most of the guys are just wishing they could figure out how to make a cool female friend of their own.

Girl Talk

"It's important for a guy to be brave enough to stand up for God. Because God is the most important person in his life, and if he won't stand up for God, he'll never stand up for me."

—Amy Roberts, 15
Hesperia, California

"True Christian girls find true Christian guys irresistible! A strong faith in God that shows in the way you handle everyday situations and relate to people around you is the most important characteristic we Christian girls are looking for in a friend."

—Paula van Rhyn
New Zealand

Brianna just told your biology class that she believes the Bible's account of God creating the earth. Now you're headed to lunch and Mo' (that's short for More Bigger Than You) is ripping her for her "stupid" beliefs. Whoa! It's gettin' ugly! You . . .

A feel bad and don't laugh. But you don't say anything either. Better that Brianna looks like a dork than you, right?

B sidetrack Mo' with a compliment on that great QB sack in last week's game.

C tell Mo', "Hey, leave her alone. It took guts to stand up for what she believes. Besides, I believe the Bible too."

You just got your driver's license, and Julie said yes when you offered to take her to the youth group moviefest. As you head from her front door toward your newly "acquired" (as in "borrowed from Dad") wheels, you . . .

A leave Julie standing on the porch and bolt for the bumper to scrub off that smudge of mud.

B beep the keyless entry and head straight for the driver's side.

C escort Julie to the passenger side, where you open her door and close it behind her.

! girl talk

"I think a guy should be a gentleman, not just to his girlfriend, but to all the girls. Most importantly, he has to be a dedicated Christian."

—Meredith Ramsey, 14
Graham, Texas

CHIVALRY DEFINED

Chivalry is a funny word. You've probably heard it in history class when the teacher was talking about knights and medieval times. You know, when guys in suits of armor rode around on horses jousting and fencing and acting like gentlemen to defend women's honor.

Okay, so some old knights-of-the-round-table movies make bowing to the ladies and dueling to defend some princess-chick's honor look kind of cheesy. But just 'cause it's an old word doesn't make chivalry—or at least its basis—obsolete. When it comes down to it, chivalry is all about respect.

And it's even a biblical concept.

No, there are no knights in the Bible, but there is Jesus. He treated women with respect and dignity in a day when females were pretty much second-class citizens. Also, check out 1 Peter 3:7 and Ephesians 5:25. In both verses Paul gives husbands some pretty steep responsibilities when it comes to treating their wives: be considerate, treat them with respect, and even more, love them as Christ loved the church—talk about the ultimate in self-sacrifice and service!

No, you don't have a wife yet. (You'd better not.) But you're learning how to relate to girls and what qualities are important to you in a girl. Most likely, you'll someday put it all together and find the girl whom you'll love as your life partner. That is, if you treat her with respect. Now is the time to practice.

clue no. five

Girls go gaga for guys who are thoughtful and courteous. Opening doors for her shows that you're putting Julie first, which shows that you respect her. It even demonstrates an attitude like Jesus'—willing to serve others.

clue no. six

Nothing impresses a girl more than sticking up for her—except maybe being confident enough to stand up for what you believe, especially your faith.

HOW?

Basically, treat girls like they're important and be willing to consider what's important to them. Here are some examples:

- Listen to her.
- Open a door and let her go through first.
- Keep that award-winning belch quiet around her.
- Compliment her (and really mean it).
- Compliment her on something even deeper than how she looks. Tell her you noticed that kind deed or thoughtful action.
- Carry her books to class.
- Open her car door before hopping in on your own side.
- Tell her she played well even though they lost.
- Lead a prayer at your lunch table.
- Ask how her day is going.

and the winner is . . .

Get out a calculator and give yourself five points for every **C** you chose. Tally two for every **B**. The **A**'s? Duh! Every **A** earns you nada, zip, zero, nothing. You're lucky we don't subtract points for those dorky answers. If your Girl Quotient is . . .

24 or more: Congratulations, young G.Q. Jedi! You've shown great wisdom with women. Keep respecting 'em. Your future wife will be happy you did.

18-23: Pretty cool, Casanova. You've got some good ideas when it comes to girls. Pay a little more attention when you're chillin' with the chicks and you'll be a G.Q. master before you know it.

10-17: You're smack in the middle, Malcolm. But there's still hope. Watch for *Breakaway's* "What Girls Think" columns. Read them with a female buddy and get her tips for aiming for the G.Q. top.

Less than 10: Thanks for playing, but you've ranked as a G.Q. Grinch—complete with a heart four sizes too small. Your consolation prize is a trip to the *Brio* mag Web site (www.brio.mag) before it's too late for you.

chapter eleven: GIRLFRIENDS OR GIRL FRIENDS?

Boy meets girl. Okay, so what then? You're ready to talk to them? Check. Know how to respect them? Check. You understand them? Check. Yeah, right. So what are you gonna do with them?

I mean, what's this whole guy/girl thing about, anyway? Where's it headed? Friendship? Love? Romance? Relationship? Marriage, eventually? But what are you gonna do with all these feelings you've got about the opposite sex right now? You know, the feelings that make you want to do more than just talk to girls—wanting to have a girlfriend or wanting to hold hands and kiss.

How you choose to deal with those feelings and the path you pick for dealing with them can affect the rest of your life. Now is the time to make those choices.

SURVIVING A CRUSH

It comes on like the flu. Your palms sweat. You get chills and the shivers. Your face feels hot and your mouth dry. Tunnel vision blurs your eyes. And when she comes around, you act delirious, slurring your speech—what few words you can get out.

Your heart also pounds, and you may find yourself writing love poetry and her initials all over your book covers. You know this is it: love. True love. Forever. You can see it now: You and Mrs. You, with two or three mini-yous and a really cool dog, staring into each other's eyes and drinking milk shakes together for the rest of eternity.

HEY! Wake up! Sorry to burst your dream bubble. But it's not gonna happen. It's totally common during the teen years to have strong feelings and emotions about girls. Your body and emotions are developing and changing more than they ever will in life. It's like somebody turned the faucet on full blast, but they keep changing the hot and cold. One day, all you can do is daydream about Lisa; the next day, she's more like a nightmare.

Don't worry. It's normal. This is the time to learn about girls and figure out what qualities are important to you. The trick is to not let your emotions totally control you.

How to Crushproof Your Heart

These tips will keep your emotions from running away with you and help you keep a balanced perspective.

- Remember that you're still young; you've got plenty of time before marriage and a lot to learn before then.

- Realize that you probably won't meet your future wife in junior high or high school.

- Learn from your feelings. Get to know Stacie, if you're interested in her, but keep it on a friendship level.

- Talk with somebody older and wiser about your crush feelings. He'll be able to give you some insight to tell if you're crushing or more.

No Means No

When a girl says she doesn't like you like that, she means she doesn't like you like that. Don't take it as a total rejection. Instead, be content to have a great friendship with a cool girl. You'll still get to hang out with her and do stuff in groups. What an awesome chance to learn more about women!

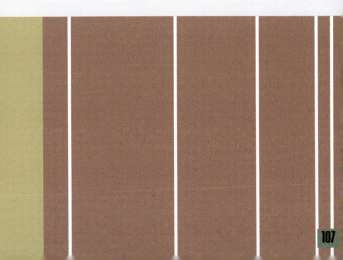

DIGGIN' DATING OR CHOOSING COURTSHIP?

You've probably heard of the debate on how to approach relationships. Maybe you've even been a big proponent of one side or the other in dating versus courtship. There are *Breakaway* readers who fall on both sides—and everywhere in between— the debate.

Dating has grown to become our culture's normal practice—you know, the dinner and a movie thing. You get up the nerve, stutter out an invitation for her to hang out only with you for a few hours, drive over to pick her up, laugh and blush a lot because you're both nervous, watch a flick, play miniature golf, go to the concert, or whatever, take her home, giggle some more, tell her you had fun, pump your fist and say "Yes!" to yourself after she closes the door, then grin and float all the way home.

Sure, it can be different for every guy. Some guys ask a girl out every once in a while, maybe even just once a year—or less. Others casually treat a different girl to some fun every so often. Some get totally wrapped up in a relationship, only to focus their total attention on another girl two weeks later . . . and so on and so on. Plenty take it to the "going out with," "going steady," or "going together" with a new-girlfriend-every-month pace. And there are guys who aren't ashamed to bring a girl along on that family ski day at the lake.

DATEVILLE 12

Courtship has made a place for itself as the antidating practice. Though it can have as many variations as dating, its basics usually include group-only activities, no exclusive relationships until marriage, lots of parental involvement, and little or no physical affection.

Courtship might mean that before you spend much time with a girl, your parents meet her and get a feel for who she is. Maybe they ask her some questions about her faith, her family, her goals, her interests. Or on the other hand, maybe the girl's parents ask you those questions.

It might sound intimidating, but the goals of courtship center around keeping God's big picture in mind and keeping the highest standards for purity.

Better?

Does dating dominate courtship? Or does courtship conquer dating? That's up to you and your parents. There are solid, committed, godly guys who do both. Whatever you practice, or plan to, the issue is an important one to think, pray, and talk to your parents about. Mom and Dad may have some strong views and set the standard for you. Or they may just want to look at the pros and cons and together set some guidelines for your intergender involvement. Together you can look at your personality, strengths, weaknesses, maturity level, and any other factors that might make a difference in the decision.

goals with girls

Whatever route you take, dating or courtship, there are some absolute—and common—goals to shoot for:

Godly relationships. Staying focused on Jesus in all your relationships is top priority. If a friendship or romantic relationship is dragging you away from God, it's time to call it quits.

Sexual purity. Purity is about more than just staying back from that forbidden line; it's a whole mind-set. It's staying as far away from going outside of God's standards as you can and literally protecting your sexual innocence. There's a lot of responsibility that comes with a relationship: to God, the girl, your family, her family, her future husband, your future wife, yourself. For more on this one, check out chapter nine.

Friendship. God has placed a high importance on our human relationships. They give us a chance to reflect His relationship with us. Our interaction with other people can teach us a lot—about others and ourselves. When it comes to girls, you can't have too many she-friends. Most of the best marriages are built on a solid foundation of friendship.

Group fun. Whether you've got a girlfriend or you go solo, you can't beat group activities. They keep the pressure—not to mention the temptation factor—low, let you get to know and interact with lots of different girls, and just plain multiply the possibilities for fun.

WHY DO YOU WANT A GIRLFRIEND?

So there's this girl. Yeah, we know: She's fun, pretty, spiritually strong, and a good friend. You love hanging out with her, and you've started wondering about taking things to the next level—you know, a relationship. But why?

It sounds like you've got a good thing going. You know each other well. You have fun hanging out together without the awkwardness of being a couple. And you're getting great practice in learning how to relate to the opposite sex.

So in all your deep contemplation, ask yourself these questions:

- *Why do I want this girl friend to become my girlfriend?*
- *How would bringing romance into our friendship improve things?*
- *Am I sensing that she wants me to be more than a friend?*

STICK WITH FRIENDSHIP IF . . .

. . . your only motive is to have a cool label to throw around: *girlfriend* instead of *friend who's a girl*.

. . . you catch yourself thinking that being "girl-less" from a romantic standpoint means being less of a guy.

. . . your other friends are pressuring you into something that shouldn't be.

. . . your hormones are taking over your brain (a desire to kiss is not a good enough reason to want a girlfriend).

SHE LIKES ME, SHE LIKES ME NOT ▌▏▎▍▌▎▍▏▎

Lots of girls are friendly. They say hi and nice things like "Cool shirt" and "Glad you came to youth group." So, how can you tell if she really LIKES you?

Does she go out of her way to be near you? You know, like when you're sitting with the guys at youth group and she just happens to be in the chair behind you—all the time.

Do you sense she's making an effort to talk to you? Is she asking you lots of questions—genuine questions about your life—and trying to get to know you?

Is she flirting with you? Like joking around, grinning lots at you, punching you playfully, staring dreamily at you when she thinks you're not looking.

reality check—or cash

TV may tell you that big bucks impress babes, but in real life, a girl worth getting to know wants to see that you're willing to work hard, spend wisely, and put some thought into who she is and what she likes. Fancy cars and flashy toys may grab attention, but only the kind that's as shallow as your reflection on that shiny chrome bumper. A relationship deep enough to last has to be built on a deep foundation.

DO'S AND DON'TS OF THE ASK-OUT

Don't . . .

- ask your best friend to ask her best friend's best friend to go out with you. Whew! No telling who'd end up saying yes.

- ask her by e-mail or instant message.

- approach her in the cafeteria and say, "You. Me. Friday night's basketball game."

- hire a singing telegram to ask her out or deliver a singing telegram yourself.

Do . . .

- be yourself.

- think ahead about what you want to say.

- be specific about what you're asking her to do.

- ask her at a time when she's alone.

- pray, psyche yourself up, take a deep breath, smile, and say something like "Hey, my friends and I are going to the football game Saturday night. Would you like to join us? My treat."

HOW TO BREAK UP

So you're the one who wants to end the relationship, huh? If you've been on the receiving side of getting dumped, you know how painful it can be. Here are a couple of tips:

- Have the talk in person and in private. It would be embarrassing for her if a dozen of her friends are with you.

- Be honest. You could say something like "You're a very special person. I just don't think a dating relationship is right for us. I'd like for us to be friends, but let's take some time to let things cool down."

WHAT TO DO **ON A DATE** (OR COURT)

When it comes to what you do when you're out with that special girl, creativity is the key; biblical—and legal—guidelines are the only boundaries. Aside from the boundaries, if you can think it, you can do it. Most girls like to see that a guy has spent some time thinking about their time together. Dinner and a movie? Come on. How original is that? Besides, how can you really get to know a person while sitting in a dark theater and staring at a screen? Here are some ideas that are great either with a group or one-on-one. Use these for starters, then jot down 10 or 12 ideas of your own.

- Stop by the thrift store, buy the ugliest clothes you can find, then hit the mall or bowling alley.

- Go hiking.

- Go to the zoo.

- Shoot home videos with all your friends.

- Organize a youth group football, basketball, volleyball, you-name-it game.

- Go in-line skating.

- Cook dinner for your, or her, family.

- Go people-watching.

- Have a progressive dinner with all your friends: Eat one course at one house, then move on to the next for more food.

- Attend a school play.

- Stop off at a coffee shop.

- Go skateboarding in the park.

- Organize a candlelight dinner in the park—for 10!

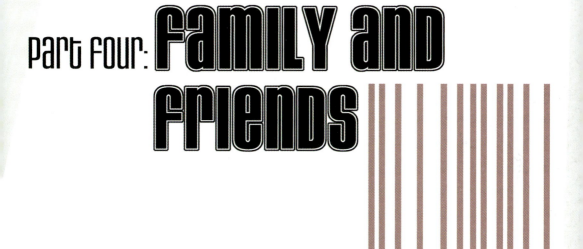

part four: FAMILY AND FRIENDS

Face it: Parents don't always make sense. Minutes after they said you're not old enough to do something, they tell you to grow up and act your age. What's the point of that?

Going through teen times is like taking a dog on a walk with a long leash. (Okay, we just compared you to Rex, but hear us out.) You can go along happy as you please for a while, but every so often, the walker is going to give a honkin' yank on that choke chain and the pup's going to remember who's running the show. Maybe the bowwow is headed off in a direction the walker doesn't want him to go (like into a busy street). Maybe he's caught a glimpse of an attractive little Doberman/pit bull combo plate—but the owner doesn't want him to turn into Puppy Chow.

FACT: Life in any household can feel more like a kennel—especially with that choker gripping your neck! That's why these next few pages are packed with vital family survival secrets, like tips on making peace with your parents, smoothing out those Tuesday night fights, and avoiding a trip to the pound for sibling homicide. So grab a snack, find a comfortable chair, and dive in!

WHY PARENTS SOMETIMES BUG YOU

So, what makes those mild-mannered parent types yank your chain? Problems usually come from the following issues:

- control
- safety
- trust
- expectations
- relationships

CONTROL

Control basically means "Who's in charge?" The bottom line, as long as you live at home, is one you may not want to hear, but it's this: Mom and Dad are in charge. Hopefully, you will be able to gain greater independence as you show maturity and responsibility, but it's in your best interest to recognize that the owner of the house is the one who sets the rules. There's a part in the Bible that talks about this (sort of). You remember that guy who gave his employees some money to take care of? A couple of them put his money to work and earned more money for the boss. As a result, they were given greater responsibilities (Luke 19:11-27). That story may have been talking about possessions, but the fact translates into a teen's life, too: If you are faithful in the little things, you have more chances to be faithful in the big ones.

safety

Overprotective parents can really bug teens. From the first time they told you not to touch a hot stove or to run with scissors, you've realized that they want you to be safe, and hopefully, you don't touch hot stoves or run with pointy things. Understand that worry is part of parents' DNA. When you are out riding in a car or driving one, Mom and Dad feel a certain level of anxiety. So, what can you do about it?

- Keep them informed about where you're heading.
- Touch base if plans change.
- Make wise choices about your activities.
- Let them get to know your friends.

Ultimately, isn't it better to have parents who care about you than some who don't love you enough to worry about you?

trust

Sometimes parents' concern for safety makes it seem that they don't trust you. But at other times, you've done something significant to break that trust, and then it seems that what might be a single failure affects every decision they make about you.

expectations

Let's be honest. Some parents try to live their lives through their children. They expect the teens to enjoy the same things they did when they were kids—whether it be sports, drama, or school—and they expect them to have at least as much success. How do you deal with this sort of pressure? First of all, be honest with your parents. If you don't have any interest in being the football player of the year, don't put yourself through a guilt trip or a miserable experience in trying to meet someone else's expectations. Do you see your real talent in the arts? Then go for it. Put forward your best effort where you've got the greatest chance of being successful. At the same time, taking this approach doesn't let you off the hook for schoolwork. Your parents have the right to expect that you will also put forward your best effort in school.

relationships

For the early part of your life, your parents had an incredible amount of influence over you—what you did, how you dressed, what you believed. As you entered the teen years, that influence began to be threatened as you developed more independence. Whether you like it or not, you probably find yourself paying more attention to what your friends do now than to what your parents do. (And the same is true for your friends, by the way.) The big PP (peer pressure) is starting to sway you one way or another.

So, how do you keep your friendships from running your relationship with Mom and Dad onto the rocks? One way is to let the "opposing forces" meet. Hopefully, you make good choices in selecting your friends. If Mom and Dad can see that the guys and girls you're running with are solid kids, ones who can be a good influence on you, chances are good that they will feel more comfortable in loosening up those reins.

HOW TO EARN BACK YOUR PARENTS' TRUST

Truth—Acknowledging the truth that you made a mistake is the first step.

Responsibility—Once you've admitted that you did something wrong, take the responsibility to make it right and to avoid future bad decisions.

Understanding—Recognize that your parents are disappointed in you and understand that they're not just punishing you.

Submission—Although it's an old-fashioned word, submitting yourself to your parents' authority and accepting their decision can help the entire situation.

Time—Realize that once people are disappointed, it takes some time for them to be convinced that they won't be disappointed in the same way again.

CONFLICT **CONTROL** ▌ ▏▏▏▏ ▏▏ ▏ ▏

Since we've agreed that parents sometimes bug you (and it would probably be healthy to admit that you bug them from time to time, too), how do you handle the times when it happens? Being able to deal with conflict is one of those incredibly important lessons that can make a difference for your whole life.

Remember when we talked about walking the dog on a leash? Well, this time you're the walker—and your temper is the dog. You've got to learn to keep it under control. Sure, there are times when you will lose it, and often the "lose it" times will be around your family. But keeping a minor skirmish from becoming a bloody battle depends on making plans ahead of time, setting rules that everybody agrees to follow.

seven rules for fighting fair

1. Focus on the disagreement, not on the other person's personality. If you really want to solve something, the disagreement has to be at the center of the conversation.

2. Provide time to cool off. Keep an eye on the gauge that measures how upset you (or the other person) are getting. As the temperatures rise and the pressure builds, it might be a good idea to go to separate rooms (or even counties) and think about options and alternatives instead of just wading into war.

3. Avoid sarcasm. One of the easiest ways to do battle is to make fun of someone else, but it's also one of the most damaging. Snotty remarks have a tendency to hurt others deeply, and the wounds will keep on giving pain long after the issue has been settled.

4. Don't bring up unrelated issues, like the last time that your dad let you down. As tempting as they may be, low blows don't contribute to resolving a conflict. In fact, the person you are arguing with probably has plenty of your past failures in reserve, and you'd rather forget those!

5. Figure out what the problem is. Is it a question of personal preference (like music) or of right and wrong (like you broke curfew and didn't even call)? Are you defending yourself in spite of the fact that you know you were wrong, or are you just trying to explain the extenuating circumstances? Are you trying to convince Mom that you will clean up that room as soon as you get back from playing tennis and that, if you do it beforehand, it will be too dark to play?

6. Understand what you hope to gain. You've probably been in situations where you "win" the argument, but the damage done to the relationship outweighs the momentary triumph. Sometimes you can find that whether or not the person changes his mind, your primary goal is to be understood. And whether he agrees with you or not, everyone can come out a winner if understanding takes place.

7. Decide when to walk away. Some issues are beaches worth dying on (like our Christian faith), but others simply are not. Weigh the costs. Giving in is not the same as giving up. But if you do choose to walk away, don't take a grudge with you and don't lock your resentment up for a later sneak attack.

"Why do I get blamed for EVERYTHING?!" you scream. Your mom crosses her arms and locks eyes with you. "Watch your tone, young man," she says in a low, stern voice. "You're not ALWAYS blamed, but you are the oldest in this family—and you know better. I want you to set a good example."

Suddenly, your little brother, who had taken cover behind your mom earlier, secretly gets your attention, sticks out his tongue, then grins from ear to ear. "Did you see that?" you gasp. "'Maggot' is doing it again."

"Oh, give it a rest," your mom responds. "Why can't you two get along? Why do you insist upon turning our house into a battle zone?"

You gasp again. Just before slamming your bedroom door, you launch one last missile: "Not only is 'Maggot' treated better, but you and Dad let him get away with murder."

Once inside your room, you flop on your bed and bury your face into a pillow. You're full-tilt angry—and are convinced that your parents conceived your little brother just to spy on you.

"He's like a miniature KGB agent," you grumble to yourself. "Just when I thought I could trust him, he tells Mom what I did last week—and I get grounded for the next three years. And as Mom pronounces punishment, that ever-so-faint smile plays across Maggot's lips. Oh, if I could just get my hands on those lips."

anger—god's way

Does our scenario hit home? Does it make you feel ticked? We're sure you're nodding your head yes, because scenes like this are played out a zillion times a day in households coast to coast.

And it's not just pesky brothers who get us steamed. In any given day, lots of stuff can push our internal "Anger Button": parents, teachers, friends, hunger . . . lack of sleep. Believe it or not, anger is a normal emotion—and there's even a right and wrong way to get mad.

Even though some people feel it's unchristian to express anger, you may be surprised to find the Bible actually offers guidelines on getting angry the right way. After all, being a Christian doesn't mean life is always great. Like other guys, you flunk tests, spill grape juice on your new white T-shirt, and get into disagreements with your friends.

So the next time the volcano is close to erupting inside you, remind yourself of what God's Word says. In Ephesians 4:26-27, Paul says, " 'In your anger, do not sin': Do not let the sun go down while you are still angry, and do not give the devil a foothold." Anger isn't the sin. It's what that anger can lead to if we don't head it off with God's help.

The question is, how can you get angry at someone and not sin? Getting angry means blowing your top, saying things you'll regret, and even hitting someone—doesn't it?

While all those are ways to express your anger, they're not the best ways. There's actually a threefold strategy to getting angry the right way.

Understand that it's okay to be angry sometimes. Certain people (like a pesky little brother) and situations (like getting grounded for missing curfew) are bound to make you mad. Just be sure you're getting angry for the right reason. Let's look at a biblical example.

Several times during His ministry, Jesus became angry with the scribes and Pharisees. Why? Because they taught people to follow the wrong path to God and thus led those people straight to the gates of hell. "You appear to people as righteous but on the inside you are full of hypocrisy and wickedness," Jesus told them in Matthew 23:28.

Our Lord spoke angrily in order to change this situation and show people the true way to God—through Himself. Jesus knew what was important enough to get angry about (where people would spend eternity) and what wasn't (like when the scribes and Pharisees came down on Him because of some of the guys He hung out with).

BE ANGRY BUT DO NOT SIN

While most guys know how to get angry, it's this second step they need to work on. Express your anger the right way. The silent treatment, screaming matches, and slugfests don't accomplish anything. If something is important enough to get angry about, then it's important enough to resolve. Try this:

- Shift your focus away from the emotion and concentrate on dealing with the situation as Jesus would. You may need to harness a burst of energy and resist the urge to let emotions rule. Pray. Ask God for help in those volatile moments.

- Instead of staying in a fit of rage, channel your anger into constructive action. Work out a deal with your brother that new CDs are off-limits for two weeks. After that, they may be borrowed with permission and with reciprocation. So next time it's his turn to buy the CD, and you get to borrow it when two weeks are up. Use your anger to find a workable solution instead of letting angry words or actions create a bigger problem.

DON'T LET THE SUN GO DOWN ON YOUR ANGER

Quickly settle whatever has you mad. When you sit and stew about a situation, the whole thing can grow bigger than the Goodyear blimp. Borrowing a tape without permission will suddenly remind you of every wrong your brother ever committed. Now you are dealing not only with the problem at hand but with another list of grievances as long as your arm. The wise thing to do if you're angry is to deal with it—quickly.

communication tips ▌▐ ▌▐ ▌▌ ▐ ▌

Okay, so maybe you aren't in the midst of a major battle, but you've got something you want to get across to your parents. The guys are having an overnighter at a friend's house next Saturday—just hanging out and watching (appropriate) movies. You're not sure how Mom and Dad will respond, and you'd really like to be heard. Your best shot at having them understand what you're trying to say is to tap in to the 10 terrific T's of teenager talking.

1. **Think about what you're going to say** ahead of time. Plan out the positive points of what you are suggesting and anticipate objections they may raise.

2. **Target your ultimate goal** and see if there are any negotiable points that can help you reach it.

3. **Keep your temper under control** no matter what happens. Losing it will probably mean you'll lose your chance of getting what you want.

4. **Check out the most effective timing** for this discussion. Right when your dad walks in the door from work or while your mom is trying to get your little brother ready for bed are not the best times.

5. **Be thoughtful and considerate** as you hear any arguments your parents may have about your plans.

6. **Engage in a two-way conversation.** Let them ask you any questions about the evening, who's coming, and what you're planning to do.

7. **Talk, don't yell.** Even if you get frustrated, make sure that this remains a discussion rather than an argument.

8. **Engage your parents as teammates,** letting them know that you want to work with them to get this arranged. Seek for areas of negotiation, like an assurance that you'll still make it to church wide awake the next morning.

9. **Keep an eye on the tone you use.** If you become demanding or disrespectful, you might as well call the guys right now to tell them the evening won't work.

10. **Once the conversation is over,** regardless of the outcome, be thankful that God has given you parents you can talk with—and show that appreciation to them, too.

Any home has its conflicts and its times of turbulence—especially homes with teenagers. But remember that once you're through the teen years, your family will still be your family. When you look back from that perspective, make sure that the wins and losses are forgotten and that you can still look at your parents with love and respect. After all, even if you yank on your dog's chain to keep him out of the street, he still loves you, doesn't he?

WHEN FAMILIES FRACTURE

If God really cares, then why have all these bad things happened to me?

If God really cares, then why do I feel so alone?

If God really cares, then why is my family so messed up?

Casey jotted the questions at the top of a sheet of notebook paper—just below the title "The Worst Year of My Life!"

The stressed-out 16-year-old had made a commitment to Christ at camp a few years back, but lately he wondered if God had given up on him. It was the perfect essay topic for his fifth-period English assignment.

Throughout the year, a lot of bad things had happened to Casey: His parents decided it was time for a change of scenery and moved the family to a small town halfway across the state (which meant leaving his friends). Then he nearly flunked out of his new school, and his dad walked out on his mom, little sister, and him.

Casey leaned back in his chair and squeezed shut his eyes. *God, if You really do care, I need to know it right now. I can handle a crazy move and some bad grades. But I can't deal with my parents' divorce.*

HELP!

COPING WITH DIVORCE

When the Bible talks about marriage, it talks about two people becoming "one flesh." When flesh rips apart, it causes pain, deep wounds, and some pretty nasty scars. Just ask Casey.

Can you relate to his pain? Has your family been ripped apart because of divorce? If so, you're not alone. While there isn't an easy way to get through the pain, there are a few things you can do to begin the healing process. Here's a good place to start:

1. **Remember that feelings aren't bad, but your response to them can be.** If you haven't yet experienced this, over the next several months you're going to feel every possible emotion: anger, resentment, self-pity, despair. You cannot control what you feel, but you can control what you do with those feelings. It's one thing to feel angry about your parents' divorce; it's another thing to dwell on that anger so it takes root and grows into hatred (see Ephesians 4:26-27, 31-32).

2. **Don't get burned by bitterness.** Get this: Bitterness is like a sour ball. The more you suck on it, the more it starts to burn your tongue, wrinkle your mouth, pucker your face, and make your eyes water. There's only one way to deal with bitterness: Spit it out (Ephesians 4:31). The good news is that you have a heavenly Father who will never leave you or forsake you. The bad news is that our parents on earth aren't quite as perfect. They make mistakes. Sometimes they do rotten wrongs.

The place to start in forgiving others is to realize we have ALL broken promises and hurt others. We can't really understand that unless we realize the hammer was in our hands that day 2,000 years ago when the nails were being pounded into the hands and feet of Jesus.

As you know, instead of being bitter, God responded with grace and mercy. Grace, because He has given us what we don't deserve, and mercy, because He didn't give us what we do deserve.

3. **Don't rush the healing process.** Ripped flesh takes time to heal. It's not like a slightly sprained ankle. You can't just walk it off. Get out of the game and give that wound some attention.

Maybe you're embarrassed and want to act like everything's cool. Maybe you think that a really good Christian would be able to keep a 150-watt grin on his face and tell people he's "doing really great." You don't need to do any of that.

Just be real, and understand that this kind of injury takes time to mend.

4. **Don't go through this alone.** You'll need to talk through some of your sadness with a trusted adult. Find a good friend, a counselor at school, or one of your pastors at church and talk to him so you can let off some steam. Let him know what's going on—not just in your house, but in your head. You may want to be brave and keep all this stuff bottled up inside. However, you won't be able to bear that kind of pressure very long.

5. **Choose to be a victor and not a victim.** It's lousy when a family fractures, but it's a choice that's out of your hands. All you can do is choose how to respond to this divorce.

You could shut down your other relationships and decide that love and life are just too risky—that you are going to live a safe, self-contained, lonely little life.

Or you could say, "Lord, use this pain in my life to make me more of the man You want me to be. Teach me about love. Teach me about commitment. Teach me about compassion and forgiveness. Teach me how to be sensitive to other people who are going through the same thing."

If you go into this thing with that kind of prayer, you might look back on this divorce someday and, instead of seeing it as a battleground where you lost your family, you might see it as a holy ground where you discovered just how real God can be.

Fifteen-year-old Matt of Franklin, Tenn., was devastated when he learned that his parents were getting a divorce. But instead of being a victim, he was determined to be a victor. Listen to how he dealt with his family's painful fracture: "Don't hold it all in. That's what I did at first. Sure divorce is bad and all, but there are a lot worse things that can happen to families. You can get through it—eventually. I mean, good stuff can come from the worst situations.

"But even though it's important to open up," he continues, "you shouldn't go around pouring your heart out to just anybody. That can be awkward. Instead, find at least one trustworthy person whom you can talk to. For me, it was my dad."

6. **Never lose hope.** Regardless of the trials we encounter in life, we must believe that God really is there, and that He truly cares for us. We must trust despite what we feel. He has our best interests at heart—as only a Father can. Lean into the truth of God as never before. Don't even entertain the notion of giving up. If you lose hope, you end up leaning into despair.

But let's be honest, saying this is easier than living it out.

Having the ability to trust God when your world is full of chaos is truly a miracle. But it's a miracle of our choosing. We have to take a step of faith—and let God do the rest. He actually empowers us to trust, and He gives us a measure of faith. Imagine that! We can't even have faith unless He gives it to us.

It's as if we close our eyes and lean back—and just believe that He is going to catch us. It's not something we can manufacture, or something we can predict. We just have to believe that we're not going to bust our heads on the concrete.

the Healing Path:
a Checklist for reaching out

Got a friend whose family just fractured? Here are some ways you can help.

Understand that divorce is like death. It involves loss and the feelings of abandonment.

Keep in mind that people in grief say things they don't really mean. Don't be easily offended at what your friend may say. Continue to stand by him and support him even when it may get tough.

Give him time to grieve. The grief process takes months, even years, to pass through. But at the same time, get help if you suspect that your pal is stuck in depression or anger.

Encourage him to talk. If not to you, get him to open up to your pastor, a trusted relative, or even a Christian counselor.

Listen to the same story again and again— as many times as he needs to tell it.

Encourage his friends to continue hanging out with him at school. If it is appropriate, tell them, "He doesn't have leprosy; he's just hurting. Keep your house open to him, too."

Help him to get on with his life—which means helping him to get involved in his usual activities: hobbies, clubs, sports activities, drama, band.

Offer a little extra help if he is having problems with schoolwork. As you are well aware, when a person is grieving, it's hard to concentrate on history, math—even P.E.

Pray for him. Ask God to give you ideas to help.

Touch is especially important to a person who's hurting. A loving embrace can communicate more strongly than words.

Get him involved in strenuous physical activities. Getting really tired physically often takes away emotional pressure.

POWER OF THE PACK ▌ ▌ ▐ ▌

Friends sometimes treat each other more like Larry, Moe, and Curly than like friends. Leave it to your buddies to do dumb things at the worst possible moments. But you wouldn't have it any other way, right? You take a few jabs and risk some bruises now and then, 'cause friendship's important.

When push comes to shove, most friends stick with you better than the gooiest slice of pepperoni pizza. Your buddies also help you blast boredom. And whether or not you realize it, they help you grow and learn more about yourself. Sometimes the only way to figure out what you're really thinking or feeling is to talk things out with a friend. And when you're with the guys, you can be yourself—even if it includes belching.

FRIENDSHIP DEFINED ▌ ▌ ▌ ▐ ▌ ▌

\FRIEND\

Webster's definitions for *friend* include these:

"one attached to another by affection or esteem"

"one that is not hostile"

"one that is part of the same nation, party, or group"

"a favored companion"

A GOOD FRIEND . . .

. . . accepts you just the way you are (despite a few jabs).

. . . is trustworthy.

. . . sticks up for you.

. . . listens.

. . . really cares.

A GOOD FRIEND DOESN'T . . .

. . . constantly stab you in the back.

. . . take off when the going gets rough.

. . . use you.

. . . lie.

MAKING FRIENDS—AND KEEPING THEM

"The best way to have a good friend is to be a good friend." That's an old proverb, but it's still true today. Follow these tips toward new friendships:

Risk reaching out. Don't be afraid. Invite that guy to your house or a youth group event.

Look for the lonely. There's always someone looking for—or needing—a friend.

Always ask. Questions give a guy a chance to talk about himself. Listen to get to know him.

Start with a smile. Friendliness puts people at ease and lets them open up.

Practice patience. It takes time to build a solid friendship.

Be realistic about rejection. Not everyone will like you. Don't take it personally; your personalities just didn't click. You're fortunate to have two or three true real buds.

HOW TO HELP A FRIEND

Sometimes friends will try anything to be accepted, even by another group. Guys want to be popular. So they compromise once, then twice . . . Before they know it—*sssslip*—they're heading over the edge and right into trouble. Some think, *I gotta look cool. This may be my only chance to move up and be really popular—and happy.*

Know a buddy who's slipping? Here's how you can help:

- Talk to your parents or youth leader about your troubled friend. Get their advice first.

- Read what the Bible has to say about helping others.

- Pray. Ask Jesus to show you what to do and to use you.

- Ask if you can talk with your buddy alone. See if he'll get together with the other guys.

- Listen to what he has to say. If he asks for your opinion, be honest and give it.

- Tell him about the power of the pack—that those you hang out with will influence you for good or bad and that some aren't worth hanging out with.

- Even if he calls you names or laughs at you, keep your friendship open. What your mixed-up buddy needs most are real friends who care about him.

- Ask God to help you forgive him.

STILL SERIOUS

You've tried everything above, but your buddy keeps heading for trouble. Or maybe another friend has let you in on a serious secret—what he's considering could really hurt him or somebody else. You don't want to be a tattletale, but you know this is dangerous.

It's tough, but sometimes one of the most loving things you can do is break a friend's confidence to protect him. Talk with your parents or youth pastor. They may need to go to his parents—or even legal authorities—to let them know what's going on. Get help. Your friend may be mad for a while, but at least he'll be safe and alive to thank you later.

CLIQUES, CLUMPS, AND CATTLE

Have you ever watched a herd of cattle? Cows love to stand around, eat, and chew—and hang out in a big group. Occasionally one cow will say, "Hey, guys, the grass is greener over there. Come on." The herd follows.

Look more closely, and you'll notice clumps: smaller groups of cows that hang together like miniherds of their own.

People are the same, especially in the teen years. We hang out with the few that we have the most in common with. It doesn't take long before the rest of the herd gives us a name: brains, skaters, jocks, geeks, popular, punks, techies, druggies.

Is that a problem?

No . . . and yes.

It's normal to hang out with people with whom we have common interests, goals, beliefs, or activities. Those things naturally draw us together and give us a foundation for friendship.

The problem comes when we get exclusive, keeping only to ourselves. Sure, it's important to choose good friends who will hold us up, but God has also called us to reach out and love the world. That's how they'll see the difference of Christ in us.

Ask yourself these questions to see if you're stuck in a clique:

- *Do you talk with others who hang in different groups?*
- *When was the last time you and your buddies added a new member to your group?*
- *Do you spend more time trying to go unnoticed or watching for new guys and girls to get to know?*
- *Have you said hi in the past week to somebody you don't really know?*
- *Can you name five friends who aren't a part of your group?*

LONELINESS AND DEPRESSION: THE DIRTY DUO

Loneliness. It strikes at the strangest times. One minute we're on top of the world. Then, in the next second, we're plunging deep into a pit. We've all been there, so we have a pretty good understanding of the disappointment and pain we endure. And at times like this, we can't help wondering, *Where are all my so-called friends? What could I have done to avoid this?*

Depression. This can involve feeling sad and low for a couple of days. In serious cases, it can result from a medical condition that requires the help of a therapist. Exactly what causes you to dive-bomb from extreme joy to extreme BLAH? Again, it's part of being a teenager. (Remember, for the next few years, your emotions will bounce from extremes and will be highly cyclical.) Lots of stuff can bring on a bout with depression: Your girlfriend dumps you, poor grades, a fight with your parents or your best friend, moving and changing schools.

DEALING WITH THE DIRTY DUO

When you find yourself face-to-face with loneliness or depression, don't allow yourself to get bogged down by all the yucky emotions inside. Instead, get some perspective and take a moment to evaluate your situation.

UNDERSTAND YOUR EMOTIONS

As we've said earlier, your feelings rise and fall like a wild ride on a roller coaster. When you're lonely and depressed today, when everything seems to be going wrong and life doesn't seem to be worth living, you need to ride it out. It may not feel very good for a while, but if you ride out these emotions, you'll discover that your circumstances will change tomorrow. Your world will seem much better. Happiness will return and the depression will disappear.

ASK YOURSELF SOME QUESTIONS

- *What's making me feel so lonely? Am I anxious about something? Is some other unresolved issue at the root of my emotions?*

- *Am I not enough? Can't I find wholeness in the fact that I'm God's creation? Can't I still feel secure in my identity in Christ—even if that means being alone from time to time?*

- *What steps am I going to take to get through this loneliness?*

- *Do I feel lonely, anxious, fearful more often than most people I know? Do I need professional help to work through these emotions?*

ALLOW YOURSELF TO CRY

Don't be embarrassed by all those raw, uncomfortable feelings tangled up inside you. Go ahead—turn your eyes toward heaven, and let the tears flow. Jesus understands. He'll be right there with you.

Take a look at what author C. S. Lewis says in *Letters of C. S. Lewis* (pg. 220): "The thing is to rely only on God. The time will come when you will regard all this misery as a small price to pay for having been brought to that dependence. Meanwhile (don't I know) the trouble is that relying on God has to begin all over again every day as if nothing had yet been done."

connect with christ

Fall on your knees and pray. Pour out your heart and tell Jesus everything you're feeling—EVERYTHING! "I feel alone . . . angry, jealous, scared. HELP!" Don't worry, nothing you can say will shock the Lord or cause Him to love you any less.

When should I get help?

Talk to your parents or a trusted Christian adult when . . .

you prefer isolation to the company of friends and family. Are you spending more and more time alone? Have you lost interest in school and peers?

depression has persisted for several days in a row. Are you detached emotionally? Are you more irritable than usual? Do you appear to be increasingly tired or sullen?

low self-esteem is constantly bringing you down. Are you always down on yourself? Do you catch yourself constantly speaking negatively about your appearance or your abilities?

Handling peer fear ▌▌▌ ▌▌ ▌ ▌

Sure, some things are harmless, but what about when the pressure pounces in areas that are mean, dangerous, or downright wrong in God's eyes? Maybe it's cheating, skipping class, drugs, alcohol, or sex.

The Bible is full of examples of guys who were willing to stand up to peer pressure to follow God. Remember: Daniel risked his life to avoid eating the king's fancy foods, even when all his captured fellow countrymen did it anyway. Millions of angry Israelites—the whole country—wanted Moses' head for leading them into the desert. And do you think it was easy for Jesus to go against the flow of all the Jewish leaders who wanted to kill Him for doing so? To make it worse, He had the devil himself pressuring Him face-to-face to give in.

Is it easy? No way. Is it worth it? You bet. God is pleased and wants to bless us when we obey Him. That doesn't mean we won't get laughed at or get revenge on the jerks. Sometimes God may give us a tangible encouragement for going against the flow. But other times we might not see any reward till much later in life—or even in heaven.

getting past the pressure

So, how do you handle it when the pressure is on? It starts by preparing yourself long before the moment. Try these tips.

Get to know God. He's the best friend you can ever have, and knowing that He's standing by will help you say no to the pressure pack.

How do you do that?

Memorize Scripture. Psalm 119:11 says it best:

> I have hidden your word in my heart
> that I might not sin against you.

Worship. Praising God brings us closer to Him and helps us focus on His voice.

Get into devotions. Spending time every day reading and studying God's Word helps us get to know Him and how we can live for Him.

Pray. You talk to your human friends, right? Talk to God about your struggles, questions, desires, and pressures.

Don't stand alone. Accountability means having a friend or two who will check up on your commitment to Christ. Ecclesiastes 4:12 says single strands of rope are weak on their own, but three woven together will stay tight and strong.

Keep your eyes on the prize—see the big picture. It's tough at the moment to stand alone and say no to that beer, porn mag, or stolen answer key. But will it matter in five years what Cool Chris thinks of you? How about God? Check out Philippians 3:12-14. Focus on the finish line, not on what's around you.

Consider the consequences. It's a law of nature: Actions have consequences. And they're not always fair. Rick may party all the time and never get caught. You may get killed the first—and last—time you ride along with his drunken crew. Think about how a choice might impact your plans, your family, your future wife, and kids. Could you be in physical danger? Or risking emotional damage?

Establish a game plan. Make up your mind ahead of time why and how you're going to say no to the temptations that will arise.

guy talk

"Be an individual. It doesn't matter what others think; it only matters what God thinks."

—Christian, 17

"Confront peers up-front with reasons why you don't want those pressures in your life: God, brain cells, etc."

—Mark, 17

"Be in the right place with the right people. Then you won't get pressured as often, and when you do, you'll feel more comfortable handling it."

—Ryan, 17

"Surround yourself with Christian influences, and remember to let God control your life."

—Jeremy, 15

"Find a group of friends who can influence you positively. A real friend will encourage you rather than drag you down into doing stuff you know is wrong."

—Jeff, 16

"Relax more and find a hobby you're proud of doing and talking about. Learn to be yourself and develop your own character, rather than just taking on characteristics of your friends."

—Chris, 16

WANTED: LEADERS ▌▏▎▏▎▏▎▏▎▏

The lone figure steps forward. "No," he says quietly but firmly.

There are gasps and whispers, giggles and guffaws, even downright challenges. "You're crazy! Loser! Everybody's doing it this way, geek!"

But then, slowly, another glances around, swallows hard, sticks one toe forward—then quickly pulls it back. Finally, with one big inner surge, he steps toward that solitary one. "Umm, h-hey. I'm with you. I think you're right." Then another and another silently move forward, switching sides, making a new stand.

They knew the truth, but the crowd were so many, the pressure was so great. All they needed was a leader. All they needed was one to step out of line and say no. And they were ready to agree with him, to get behind him, to step up with support. Sure, they're still the minority, but they know, down deep inside, what is true and right—and what the ultimate Leader wants. They just needed the one.

The world is looking for a leader. That can be you.

top five **pressure points** ▌ ▌ ▌▌ ▌▌ ▌

Peer fear can cause otherwise smart Christian guys to do some pretty dumb things. And you've probably discovered there are five top pressure points that get some teens into big-time trouble: smoking, alcohol use, experimenting with pot and other drugs, cussing, and the temptation to be sexually active.

In the paragraphs that follow, we've printed some questions from real guys like you, along with some advice on how you can deflate the pressure and save yourself from future headaches—*and* heartaches.

pressure to smoke

Lately, a couple of my friends have been pressuring me to go out and smoke with them. I don't want to, but I'm afraid to say no. What should I do?

You're smart for not wanting to smoke. After all, what your buddies may see as a risky "guy thing" can end up getting pretty gross: wheezing lungs, yellow teeth, ashtray breath—a life cut short. Smoking and a healthy body just don't mix. Prolonged tobacco use can cause a host of life-threatening diseases.

The problem is, your friends are stuck on the risky guy part, which leaves you with some hard questions to consider:

What's the No. 1 thing keeping me from facing my friends and telling them I don't want to smoke?

Would I rather confront the guys and chance losing our friendship or give in and do what I know is wrong?

Do I want growth or guilt? (I'll probably always wish I had stood strong for what I believe.)

God's Word can give you the strength and encouragement you need to face your friends. Proverbs 13:20 says, "He who walks with the wise grows wise, but a companion of fools suffers harm."

It's a tough step, but you know what you've got to do: Speak up and be true to yourself and God. You may face some weirdness from the guys—like put-downs or a strain on your friendships. Yet we've discovered that most people respect those who show backbone and stand confidently for what they believe. What's more, your courage may be just the thing your buddies need right now. Your actions today may steer them away from even dumber risks in the future.

pressure to Drink

Several months ago I tried some alcohol with my friends. Since then, I've been tempted to drink again. What does the Bible say about alcohol?

It says a lot. Here are some highlights:

1. Drunkenness is completely off-limits (see Ephesians 5:18).

2. Adults are permitted to drink a little wine for health reasons (see 1 Timothy 5:23). Yet in Numbers 6:3 God instructed those who wanted to make a special vow to "abstain from wine and other fermented drink."

3. Romans 14:13-21 tells us to avoid doing anything that might cause another person to stumble. So if you openly kick back with a beer, you're telling others that it's okay to drink. But your attitude shouldn't be "Hey, this doesn't hurt me, so what's the big deal?" You need to ask, "How will this affect my friends?"

4. First Corinthians 6:12 says, " 'Everything is permissible for me'—but not everything is beneficial. 'Everything is permissible for me'—but I will not be mastered by anything."

In other words, it's not a question of "Can I drink?" It's an issue of "Should I?" Those who are wise don't see how close they can get to the edge of the cliff without falling off. Rather, they tell themselves, "If I never take the very first drink, then I won't have to worry about ever getting drunk or hurting myself and others."

Having said all this, let us remind you of what the Bible says regarding three other simple matters:

Lying to parents: Don't do it. Was drinking with your friends something you had to hide from your parents?

Disobeying parents: Don't do it. Did you have your parents' permission to try alcohol?

Disobeying the civil laws: Don't do it. If you are under the legal drinking age, you and your friends broke the law. The Bible says that is a no-no (see Romans 13:1-7).

pressure to use pot (and other drugs)

Where I live a lot of teens smoke pot. I've tried it and—I won't lie—I liked it. Is it really wrong for Christians to do this? Didn't God say in Genesis to live off the seeds of the earth?

We assume you're talking about Genesis 1:29. That's where God says, "I give you every seed-bearing plant on the face of the whole earth and every tree that has fruit with seed in it. . . ." If that's the passage, I wonder why no one showed you the last part of the verse where God says, "They will be yours for food." (Not for smoking.)

There's a whole lot more we could write about this issue—like how pot can be harmful to your life emotionally, physically, and spiritually. But there might be a simpler way. Just use the list below to see if smoking pot is okay for you as a Christian.

If you checked one or more of these statements, then you have your answer: Smoking pot is a sin.

Whether the issue is pot or some other substance that people abuse, here's a four-point strategy for staying drug-free.

1. **Get the facts straight.** "I'll try it just once—it can't hurt and I won't turn into a druggie." This is the lie of the century. Don't be fooled; drugs kill. A "high" may feel good for a little while, but the drug is poisoning your body. Take in too much of it—or keep using it—and your body breaks down and dies.

take this quick quiz (put a check next to each statement that's true)

- ☐ **It will** cause me to disobey the law.
- ☐ **It will** cause me to disobey my parents.
- ☐ **It may** possibly cause me to lie.
- ☐ **It may** be harmful to my physical body (see 1 Corinthians 6:19-20).
- ☐ **It can** potentially have the same effect on my judgment and behavior as drunkenness.

2. **Don't even get started.** The best defense against drugs is to avoid them. Don't give in—even once.

3. **Seek help.** If you have a friend who is in trouble, you've got to do more than just watch. Talk to a parent or a teacher. If you think they wouldn't get the picture, go to a coach, a counselor, or your minister.

4. **Make a pact with God.** The Holy Spirit gives us the wisdom to make good decisions, along with the strength to carry them out. The fact is, we serve a God with guts—a God who is strong and courageous.

pressure to cuss

What's the big deal about curse words? I mean, it's a guy thing. A lot of my friends, even Christian ones, swear. Curse words are just that—*words*. Where did they come from, and why do Christians condemn them?

Before we check out what the Bible says, let's crack open a Webster's and look up some definitions of the word *curse:* "to swear at; use profane, blasphemous, or obscene language against; to bring evil or injury on; afflict." (Take note of two key words used here: *against* and *afflict.*)

Now let's pop over to James 3:9-11 for some insight: "With the tongue we praise our Lord and Father, and with it we curse men, who have been made in God's likeness. Out of the same mouth come praise and cursing. My brothers, this should not be. Can both fresh water and salt water flow from the same spring?"

The fact is, words are far from harmless—especially the ones that *curse, afflict,* and *tear down*. And it's kinda obvious where they come from and why they're off-limits to Christians: SIN.

Consider this about all the words that casually fly out of our mouths:

God wants us to have no part of sinful acts—which include using bad language. He makes it clear that sin and holiness just don't mix. "But now you must rid yourselves of all such things as these: anger, rage, malice, slander and filthy language from your lips" (Colossians 3:8).

Words—especially curse words—can be deadly. They can cut open a heart and destroy a person's self-image. They can ignite a fire and drive someone to violence. The wrong kinds of words can cause incredible harm. That's why James tells us to control our tongues. (See James 3:1-6.)

Christians must use words for good, not evil. Through our words, we can promote healing. We can express God's love and show that He cares. "Do not let any unwholesome talk come out of your mouths, but only what is helpful for building others up according to their needs, that it may benefit those who listen" (Ephesians 4:29).

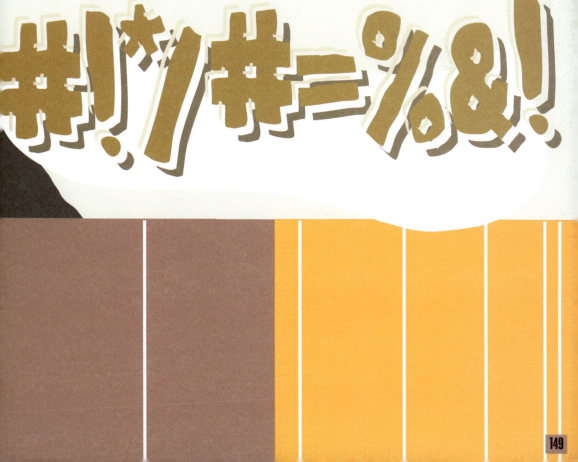

? pressure to be sexually active

A friend is having premarital sex. I've always been taught that this is wrong, but the problem is, I can't find Scripture that says this specifically. All the passages I've read have to do with orgies and sexual immorality in marriage. But if two unmarried people—both of whom consider themselves to be Christians and who have the consent of their parents—are having sex in a committed relationship, what should stop them?

!

The absence of a wedding band—that's what should stop them.

Just because Scripture doesn't *specifically* say, "Don't have sex before marriage," the Bible clearly communicates this message. And just because your friends consider themselves to be Christian—and presumably have their parents' permission to have sex—sin is sin. Like it or not, *premarital sex = sin*.

A number of passages in the Bible tell us that marriage is the right place for sex—and specifically state that extramarital alternatives are off-limits for believers. Take a look at a few:

Adultery is wrong—Exodus 20:14

Sex with a prostitute is wrong—
1 Corinthians 6:15-17

Impurity is wrong—Colossians 3:5-7

With verses such as these, do you honestly think that God would make an exception for premarital sex? Is sex outside of marriage something He considers pure and moral? Of course He doesn't.

You mentioned that your friends are having sex "in a committed relationship," hinting that this just might make it okay. Get this: Sex is designed for only one kind of committed relationship: holy matrimony. When a man and a woman have sexual intercourse, something happens to the two of them, something that changes them at the deepest level. A husband and wife are bound together *body and soul.* And this bond is never supposed to be separated. (Can you see why divorce is so devastating?)

In other words, sex isn't just physical, and it's not a trivial act that feels good for a few seconds and then is over. Sex involves a couple's body, mind, and emotions in an activity that is intended to continue for a lifetime.

If you're still not convinced, check out what Scott of Grand Rapids, Mich., has to say on this topic. He's a guy who has "been there, done that"—and desperately wishes he hadn't.

I have something important to say to every guy out there. I'm an 18-year-old who has always heard Christian views about premarital sex and the consequences of giving in. Unfortunately, I didn't listen. It seems that the whole world is telling us that sex is okay. And it is—strictly within the bonds of marriage. But instead of following God's Word, I tuned in the world and gave away my virginity.

At the time, I was convinced that having sex was the most wonderful thing in the world. Afterward, it left the girl and me with heartache. I don't mean simple hurt feelings; I'm talking about utter heartache. Not a day goes by that I don't regret that first sexual touch. Why? Because it gradually led to other things—and eventually to intercourse.

I know that God has forgiven me for my sins, but I can't help asking myself, Will my future wife forgive me? How am I going to tell her that I gave away a gift that was meant only for her? And on my wedding night, I'll have pictures of other girls in my head, which is so wrong! To treat women as most of the secular world does is absolute sin.

Fellas, I envy every one of you who doesn't know what sexual intimacy with a girl is like. If you're a virgin, you are so fortunate. I pray that you'll stay pure for marriage and that God will richly bless your marriage bed. And as much as you want sex now, remember that God has the right kind of woman in mind for you—that is, if it's His desire for you to be married. Hold strong and give your future wife the gift of your virginity.

Flip back to chapters eight and nine for much more advice on the topics of sex and purity.

CHAPTER THIRTEEN: SURVIVING THE CHALKBOARD JUNGLE ||| || |

During your four years of high school, you will spend over 4,000 hours in class. (That's assuming you make it to class.) It may be tempting to think of those 4,000 hours just as time that you have to be there. But if you actually pay attention in class, that time can produce great dividends. The payoff comes not just in grades and academic knowledge but also in increased self-discipline.

And who knows? Someday when you're facing Alex Trebek on Jeopardy, *something your third-period teacher once said may come back into your mind and help you win significant dollars!*

The truth is that school is far more than learning head knowledge; it is a training ground for characteristics and skills that can create a satisfying lifestyle, whether or not college fits into your plans.

Want to make those 4,000 hours count? Keep reading.

SUCCESS IN SCHOOL | | ||| || | |

PLANNING

One of those obsessive-compulsive teachers, Mr. T., mapped out his entire history class during the summer. The first day of class, he handed out the reading assignments, the research paper expectations, the quiz dates, the unit exam schedule—stuff that really intimidated his students.

So, what did Sample Student A do? Exactly what you might expect—he stuffed the info deep into his backpack, never to be seen again (at least without dramatic wrinkles and residue from the sandwich that his mom sent with him to be sure he had "something nourishing"). After all, Student A knew that Mr. T.

would remind him as things were coming up, and that would give him plenty of time to cram enough facts into his head to get by.

The problem was that Mr. T. had a secret life as a motorcycle rider and crashed his Harley into a tree one evening, fracturing some very important parts of his anatomy. His substitute came in, found the lesson plans, and carried on. But *on the day before* the semester-long research report was due, Sammy Subbie looked ahead and told the kids, "Oh, and by the way, I'm sure you remember the 900-page research project is due tomorrow with note cards, bibliography, and everything." Sample Student A sat there choking in his tubular steel desk.

Sample Student B, on the other hand, had taken a different approach. When Mr. T. handed out that first flood of papers, this student went through them, put the significant dates onto a big calendar, and actually started working on some of the long-range projects. By the time Sammy Subbie made the statement that sank Student A's ship, Student B was into the final revision stages and already had his bibliography ready to type up.

The moral of the story is not to get the entire semester's work done in the first week but to plan out when things fit together.

time management

Believe it or not, high school can be one of the most activity-filled seasons of your life. Classes, church activities, athletic events, drama performances, part-time jobs, club meetings, times to just hang out—all of these compete dramatically for your time and attention. For most guys, this is the period in your life when you begin to have a little more independence in how you spend your time, depending on how much freedom your parents let you have. But it's also a time that can be threatening to your success if you don't show some self-control.

The secret here is to maintain balance and flexibility. If you're playing football in the fall and Coach expects you to be at practice every afternoon until six, that's going to cut into your expendable time. You'll still want time with your friends, but depending on your exhaustion level, you may have to hold off until the weekend. Completing your schoolwork has to take a higher priority. Or maybe you have a lead role in the senior class play. Rehearsals take an increasing amount of time as you creep closer to the performance, so keep an eye on those major papers that are due right around opening night and get a start on them early.

One teacher recalls Rob, an athlete who was also a school leader. "Rob was involved in everything his freshman and sophomore years. But early in his junior year, he was so stretched out in responsibilities that he wasn't doing anything as well as he wanted. He was forced to make some decisions that were really tough because he didn't want to let anybody down. But he cut back on some involvements, focusing his primary attention on his role in student government, basketball, and his leadership in the Young Life group. That gave him more time to concentrate. While he didn't have as wide an influence as he did his first two years, he had more personal time to invest deeply with a limited number of people."

BUILD YOUR STRENGTHS

Certain fundamental abilities are essential for academic success in school. There's a reason why schools are known for the three R's: reading, writing, and 'rithmetic (although spelling must not have been important for the last two). Rare individuals are blessed with the ability to pursue multiple interests well; most of us common folks have skills in a limited area.

It's tempting to focus primarily on the subjects you like and to just get by in the others. It may be an overgeneralization to say that guys have more talent in math and science than in subjects that require strong verbal skills (English, history, languages, and communication), but it is often true. *Breakaway's* advice is to pursue those areas where you are strongest, to be sure. But don't neglect those you don't enjoy. Being able to write clearly, to read with understanding, and to communicate in both oral and written forms are talents that are essential even for engineers and scientists.

The best way to build writing skills: WRITE—and have someone else read and respond to what you write.

The best way to build reading skills: READ—and talk over what you have read with someone else so you're sure you understand what you've read.

relating to teachers

Let's take a moment to undo one commonly believed rumor: Teachers are NOT (repeat, ARE NOT) aliens from another planet. Nor are they robots with no recognizable human characteristics. In fact, hard as it may be to believe, they are human beings. And their purpose is truly to work for your benefit.

Now that they have been humanized, here are a few things NOT to do to teachers if you want to get along with them:

- Don't make fun of them.
- Don't expect them to do you favors (that doesn't mean they won't do them; just don't expect them).
- Don't question their authority in the classroom.
- Don't write out a slip sending them to the office.
- Don't fall asleep while they are talking to the class.
- Don't ask one out on a date (even if she is cute and young).
- Don't try to confuse them when the principal is in the room.
- Don't treat them like buddies.
- Don't neglect to do assignments they give because the assignments seem like busywork to you.
- Don't use church activities as an excuse even if a teacher goes to your church.

Here's the truth about teachers: You will get along with some of them and will have trouble getting along with others. You see, this is like the real world. Those of you who already have jobs realize that some supervisors are easier to please than others; some are more helpful than others; some are old, some are young; some are easygoing and others are all business. Teachers are the same way, fitting all those categories. Some (in fact, most) work hard and get a little ruffled when noneducators say, "You work only nine months a year from eight to three with all those vacations."

For students (and this will hold through into college as well), teachers are put into authority over you by God, so there are some verses in Romans that you should be familiar with and should apply to your life. Check out what Paul wrote to the Romans in chapter 13: "Everyone must submit himself to the governing authorities, for there is no authority except that which God has established. . . . Do you want to be free from fear of the one who is in authority? Then do what is right and he will commend you. For he is

God's servant to do you good" (verses 1, 3, and 4). Some take that authority much more seriously than others and hold it tightly. But whether the teacher demands respect or not, give it to him or her. This holds true whether you attend a public school or a Christian one—and home-schooled students get a double dose because of God's command to honor your father and your mother.

Anybody who's been in schools at all realizes there are some teachers in any setting who are ripe for teasing and making fun of. *Breakaway* guys, resist that temptation. In fact, whether it's a teacher or the downtrodden, victimized student with the locker next to you, making fun of anyone may get you some momentary laughs, but the long-term effects hurt. As for favors, some teachers can be taken advantage of, but doing so may not benefit you in the long run. If it happens too often, the teacher starts to regard the favor asker as irresponsible, a slacker who doesn't want to follow the rules set for the rest of the class. This can prove to be a particular temptation if you have a Christian teacher in a public school—don't get roped in.

But instead of focusing on what NOT to do to get on the good side of teachers, how can you positively approach them to contribute to your success?

- **Do your work.** Put forth your best effort instead of making excuses.

- **Ask questions.** If you don't understand something, get help from the teacher soon instead of waiting for several days or weeks. And ask questions before or after class or during a teacher's conference period. Don't interrupt the class with a question unless you think it might be something that would benefit many of your classmates, not just you.

- **Pay attention.** We're not just talking here about managing to avoid falling asleep. Pay attention to what is going on in your teachers' lives. They are people like you with good days and bad. One teacher told us, "A particular student made a dramatic impact on me when my mom was dying. I didn't make a big deal about it, but his sensitivity clued him in that I was going through a tough time. He discreetly asked me after class how I was doing—with a sincere interest. I didn't dump all my pain on him, but I felt safe to let him into my life at least a little. Knowing that he knew helped me through the next difficult couple of weeks."

- **Pray for them.** Yes, just like any other people who can make a difference in your life, teachers deserve and desire your prayers.

- **Be a leader in the classroom.** Notice that doesn't say cheerleader—doing this too much can create the image of a shmoozer or a kiss-up. But you can take the responsibility to contribute to discussions, to discourage kids who act up, to use the opportunity to team with the teacher in focusing on what is being taught.

- **Stay in touch.** Even though doing so may contribute little to your school success, keep contact with teachers who have made an impact in your life. Too often educators invest heavily into someone and have no idea what happens to him after graduation. One student waited four years to do so, but as he was graduating from college and preparing to go into teaching himself, he wrote a letter to a high school teacher who had dramatically affected him. The letter he got back was like an epistle, a charge to pursue a significant calling. That young man is no longer young, but he still has a copy of that letter—30 years later.

prayer: KNOW YOUR RIGHTS ▌▎▎▎▎ ▎▎ ▎

This chapter has talked about school success and people success. But to survive the chalkboard jungle, especially in the public schools, sometimes you need to experience faith success as well.

The press tries to communicate the idea that the campus is off-limits to any expressions of Christian faith. But do you know what? That's not true. The constitutions of both the United States and Canada protect students' freedom of religious expression. You can tell people what you believe without getting arrested!

Do you know what you can and cannot do on a public school campus?

take this QUICK QUIZ (CHECK ONE BOX PER STATEMENT)

☐ **Yes** ☐ **No** Students can pray.

☐ **Yes** ☐ **No** Students can read their Bibles.

☐ **Yes** ☐ **No** Students can form religious clubs if other noncurricular clubs exist.

☐ **Yes** ☐ **No** Students can hand out tracts, flyers, or other religious materials.

☐ **Yes** ☐ **No** Students can do research papers and speeches with religious themes.

☐ **Yes** ☐ **No** Students can be exempt from participating in assignments that are contrary to their religious beliefs.

☐ **Yes** ☐ **No** Students can discuss religious issues even when other students may overhear.

The answer to all these statements is yes—students have great freedom of religious expression even on public school campuses.

STUDENT BILL OF RIGHTS ON A PUBLIC SCHOOL CAMPUS

The right to meet with other religious students. The Equal Access Act allows students the freedom to meet on campus for the purpose of discussing religious issues.

The right to identify your religious beliefs through signs and symbols. Students are free to express their religious beliefs through signs and symbols.

The right to talk about your religious beliefs on campus. Freedom of speech is a fundamental right mandated in the Constitution and does not exclude the school yard.

The right to distribute religious literature on campus. Distributing literature on campus may not be restricted simply because it is religious.

The right to pray on campus. Students may pray alone or with others so long as it does not disrupt school activities and is not forced on others.

The right to carry or study your Bible on campus. The Supreme Court of the United States has said that only state-directed Bible reading is unconstitutional.

The right to do research papers, speeches, or creative projects with religious themes. The First Amendment to the U.S. Constitution does not forbid all mention of religion in public schools.

The right to be exempt. Students may be exempt from activities and class content that contradict their religious beliefs.

The right to celebrate or study religious holidays on campus. Music, art, literature, and drama with religious themes are permitted as part of the curriculum for school activities if they are presented in an objective manner as a traditional part of the cultural and religious heritage of the particular holiday.

The right to meet with school officials. The First Amendment forbids Congress to make any law that would restrict the right of the people to petition the government, including school officials.

To learn more, request *Students' Legal Rights on a Public School Campus* ($10 U.S.), See You at the Pole. P.O. Box 60134, Fort Worth, Texas 75115. Or call 1-817-HIS-PLAN.

part five: HOLLYWOOD SQUARES— DON'T BE ONE

"The most powerful nations are not those who have bombs, but those who control the media. That's where the battle is being fought; that is how you control people's minds."

—**Filmmaker Spike Lee**

Not all preachers stand in pulpits. Not all teachers shape minds in classrooms. And not everyone with something to sell does it in a 30-second commercial. With very little fanfare, entertainment communicates the beliefs and agendas of the people who create it. The screenwriter. The songwriter. A producer or director. And relatively few of them have a biblical worldview. But do those messages really have an impact? Absolutely!

"Every study that I've ever seen that's done by the networks, the [movie] studios, educational organizations, tell us over and over again that we are all influenced by the media we consume," says Michael Warren, an executive producer at Warner Brothers.

Of course, that's not always bad. Songs that celebrate peace, love, and strong family relationships can have a positive impact on the way people treat each other. Likewise, movies and TV shows often rally public sympathy and support for noble causes. But as members of the audience, we need to know when our buttons are being pushed. Although the entertainment industry hates to admit it, they don't always use their talents for our benefit.

a Dangerous **DOUBLE STANDARD** | | | | | | | | | |

Wheel of Fortune host Pat Sajak admits that show-biz people race to take credit for the good that comes from their work but are just as quick to distance themselves from the *bad*. It's an age-old double standard. Sajak said, "Television people have put blinders on, and they absolutely refuse—and movie people too—to admit that they can have any influence for ill in our society. You know the argument: 'We only reflect what's going on; we don't perpetuate it.' And yet not a week goes by in this town where there's not an award ceremony where they're patting each other on the back saying, 'You raised AIDS awareness' [or] 'There'll be no more child abuse thanks to that fine show you did.' The argument is you can only influence for good; you can't influence for ill. That makes no sense at all."

Buy that man a vowel! Sajak is right on the money. For good or for ill, the media is persuasive. Otherwise, the TV network lucky enough to air the Super Bowl each year wouldn't be able to demand a record dollar amount for 30 seconds of air time.

HOW FAR WILL FANS GO?

It would be easy to trot out extreme cases of kids seeing films like *Scream* or *Natural Born Killers* and copying violent acts. We could spend pages (don't worry, we won't) detailing the crimes of people who made a habit of listening to hateful music and then went out and mimicked it. In fact, school shooter Jamie Rouse admitted to listening to Morbid Angel as a way of psyching himself up to murder a classmate ("It just made me feel capable of evil. It makes you feel like you want to kill someone"). From his prison cell Rouse said, "I used to think, 'This ain't affecting me. You'd have to be weak-minded to let this stuff affect you.' And the whole time it affected me—it helped shape the way I thought. . . . All those songs and the movies that make killing look cool. They don't show in the movies what it does to those people and their families. And sittin' in prison for the rest of your life isn't fun."

Clearly, Jamie Rouse and others like him are at the far end of the spectrum. But for every lover of violent entertainment who commits a crime or mimics a dumb stunt he saw on MTV's *Jackass,* countless others are being affected in a less visible way. They're being desensitized to suffering.

Let's shift gears a second. In the sexual arena, will everyone who rents *American Pie* or watches *Friends* run out and have sex? Of course not. But a steady diet of immorality will make what's wrong seem right—or at least "normal." It can recondition our thinking and cause us to doubt the absolute standards spelled out in the Bible.

a modern parable

Once there was this guy named JoJo whose history class was studying the state capitals. Just before the bell rang one day, the teacher mentioned that Carson City was the capital of Nevada. JoJo made a mental note of it, closed his books, and went on with his day.

After school, JoJo read an article in a skateboarding mag about a cool new skate park being constructed in Nevada's "capital city" of Las Vegas. He shook it off, convinced it was a typo. Later on, he surfed through basic cable and found a show on CNN that showed a map of Nevada with a little star identifying Las Vegas as the capital. Strange. And when he popped in a CD by his favorite band, 120 Degrees Latitude, the song "Capitol Offense" blared the lyric, "We're cruisin' to Las Vegas for a party on the capitol steps." Doubt started to creep into JoJo's mind. Was his teacher mistaken?

The next day, JoJo and his classmates got a pop quiz on state capitals. What do you think he wrote down when he got to Nevada?

This fictional story is an example of how media voices can undermine God's eternal truth and cause you to stumble. For example, you may have been taught that God's plan for sexuality is *abstinence* before marriage and *faithfulness* afterward. You've made that mental note. Yet popular entertainment promotes a very different attitude. Women are prizes to be won. The question isn't "Should I wait for marriage?" but rather "How long should we date before we do it?" Characters seem to have so much fun bouncing in and out of bed, especially since there are so few consequences in the land of make-believe. Then one day you get a pop quiz. Temptation comes knocking and you have to decide what is true—the spiritual standard you read in a book or the one driven home time and time again by the amoral media with its airbrushed images and emotional gimmickry.

Colossians 2:8 warns, "See to it that no one takes you captive through hollow and deceptive philosophy, which depends on human tradition and the basic principles of this world rather than on Christ." No one is peddling more hollow and deceptive philosophy than the entertainment industry. And when worldly philosophies and morality masquerade as fun, they can penetrate our hearts virtually unchallenged.

LAS VEGAS

MEDIA AND YOUR MIND

"Its effects are measurable and long-lasting."

—Part of a landmark joint statement by the American Medical Association, the American Psychological Association, the American Academy of Pediatrics, and the American Academy of Child and Adolescent Psychiatry on the ability of violent entertainment to impact young people

KEYS to DISCERNMENT

"The Lord has assigned to each his task. I planted the seed, Apollos watered it, but God made it grow."

—1 Corinthians 3:5-6

In his first letter to the Corinthian church, the apostle Paul alluded to the way God's Word is spread and nurtured. He used a simple farming metaphor to make his point: Paul sowed; Apollos watered. Each played an important part in the grand plan of growth. Cool. Now let's take that example a step further for the purposes of exploring entertainment's impact on our personal holiness.

As we know from Jesus' parable of the sower in Luke 8, plants rarely flourish without some opposition. Like thorns. Or weeds. We could classify "weeds" as pretty much *anything* that could entangle our spirit and interfere with growth.

Okay, back to sowing and watering for a second. Your parents—as well as your church leaders—may be sowing God's Word into your life in a powerful way. And it's getting watered every week at youth group. So far, so good. Now what about the weeds? Make no mistake, they're there. What most teen guys fail to realize is that "weeds" in the form of unhealthy entertainment can spring up and choke out holiness. That includes explicit stuff, but it also includes subtle messages that can be even *more* damaging.

We've already pointed out the power of media messages. Here's the hard part: While others can sow and water in your life, only you can be the weed whacker!

r u ready 2 get radical?

A radical walk with Jesus Christ requires *discernment*. Discernment is just a fancy term for the kind of wisdom that helps us choose between right and wrong, between good and bad, between Creed's *Human Clay* and the latest CD by Slipknot. Get the picture? You're faced with decisions constantly. Wouldn't it be cool to know you're making the right ones? King Solomon thought so. In fact, he valued discernment so much that, when God said he could have anything he wanted, Solomon asked for discernment instead of money or a long life (1 Kings 3).

Spiritual insight starts with the Bible. God's Word gives us a yardstick for measuring all kinds of things—from music lyrics to video games—to see if they meet His standards. Sometimes a video box or CD cover says it all. Other times it's less obvious. Wanna be like Jesus? Then pray for discernment and ask God to give you His mind concerning popular culture.

! proper perspective

"My son, preserve sound judgment and discernment.

Do not let them out of your sight."

—King Solomon in Proverbs 3:21

THE Battle WITHIN ▮▮ ▮ ▮ ▮ ▮▮ ▮

It's important to remember that there's a battle going on inside your heart. Galatians 5:17 explains: "The sinful nature desires what is contrary to the Spirit, and the Spirit what is contrary to the sinful nature. They are in conflict with each other, so that you do not do what you want." Do you know that feeling? Have you ever seen the *Sports Illustrated* swimsuit issue staring at you from a magazine rack? Were you tempted to pick it up and flip through it? C'mon, admit it. That's the way guys are *wired*. *Sports Illustrated* knows that. The filmmakers behind teen sex comedies know that. Britney Spears knows that. The dudes who created Lara Croft know that. Still, with God's help, we don't have to give in and expose ourselves to it.

The flesh and spirit hunger for different things. The flesh has an appetite for "junk food." That could include anything from crude sitcoms and sexually preoccupied R & B tunes to gory computer games and slasher films. The spirit, on the other hand, feeds on Bible study, prayer, Christian music, hanging out with godly people, and serving others (Romans 13:14 encourages "Spirit-fed" living; Galatians 5:22 details the benefits). A lot of entertainment panders to the flesh. Lust. Greed. Vengeance. Jealousy. The more you feed that nature, the more it will be reflected in your heart.

A lot of guys make the mistake of compartmentalizing their Christian faith. In other words, an intimate walk with the Lord applies only to certain areas of their lives. *Not!* Jesus wants to be Lord of *all*. Consider Him when you buy a movie ticket. Don't shut Him out when you put on a set of headphones. If you don't think critically and Christianly about entertainment, the media will eat your lunch.

FIGHTING THE GOOD FIGHT

"Beware of going to the funeral of your own independence. The natural life is not spiritual and it can only be made spiritual by sacrifice. We go wrong because we stubbornly refuse to discipline ourselves, physically, morally or mentally. Our natural life must not rule; God must rule in us."

—Oswald Chambers,
author of *My Utmost for His Highest*

WHERE are the BOUNDARIES?

It's difficult to know what's in bounds and what's out of bounds if we base decisions on box office figures, record sales, Nielsen ratings, or what our friends think. Isn't there anything more reliable and absolute to guide those decisions? You bet there is! The Bible includes lots of verses that apply, even though it was written centuries before Buffy started slaying vampires or Tupac busted his first glock. But maybe the acid test for entertainment should be 2 Peter 1:5-8.

The author says, "Make every effort to add to your faith goodness; and to goodness, knowledge; and to knowledge, self-control; and to self-control, perseverance; and to perseverance, godliness; and to godliness, brotherly kindness; and to brotherly kindness, love. For if you possess these qualities in increasing measure, they will keep you from being ineffective and unproductive in your knowledge of our Lord Jesus Christ." Are you possessing those qualities "in increasing measure"? If not, maybe it's because so much of today's entertainment devalues things like godliness, self-control, and brotherly kindness. We need to make choices that reinforce the positive. That means eliminating messages that could undermine Christlike character.

Of course, when you put something to the test and draw a line between right and wrong, as sure as there's mystery meat in the school cafeteria, someone who disagrees will quote Matthew 7:1. They shout, "Don't judge, or you too will be judged!" as they wag a finger in your face. Ever been there? It's important to remember that, in this verse, Jesus is warning against judging others' thoughts and motives and the hidden things of the heart that only God can see. It *doesn't* mean we should ignore sin and refuse to practice discernment. When the evidence is clear, it's our responsibility to make wise judgments on our quest for holiness.

! THE RIGHT SIDE OF THE LINE

"Test everything. Hold on to the good. Avoid every kind of evil."

—1 Thessalonians 5:21-22

CHAPTER SIXTEEN: MUSIC—DISSECT THE LYRICS

"There is nothing more singular about this generation than its addiction to music."

—Allan Bloom in his best-selling book *The Closing of the American Mind*

Believe it or not, that statement was written in 1987. Yet it's as true today as ever. Your friends—maybe even you—spend an amazing amount of time listening to music. The average teen hears 10,500 hours of music between grades 7 and 12. That equals more than 14 months nonstop. And judging from CD sales, you're not just listening to it on the radio; you're also buying it. In 2001, the music industry sold a record 762.8 million albums. That's a lot of tunes!

Rap. Rock. Country. R & B. Latin. Jazz. Christian. Which ones inspire your best air guitar? More important, what do those songs say? And why does it matter?

THE POWER OF MUSIC: IT'S ALL IN YOUR HEAD

Have you ever gotten a tune stuck in your head? You only need to hear a few bars and—*zap!*—it starts buzzing around in there for hours. It could be a commercial jingle, a TV theme song, or a top-40 hit.

Maybe you heard it in a record store or at a restaurant. You wander through the mall and find yourself humming the last song that was playing on your car stereo before you turned off the engine. *Buzz, buzz, buzz.* And it's not just the music. The words rattle around in there too, and some of those words can be pretty lame when you stop to think about 'em. The point is that music tends to travel with us. Good or bad, it rarely goes in one ear and out the other.

Back before there were snowboards, guys looking for a good time in the middle of February would get their kicks "bumper hitching." The idea was that some kid would hide behind a parked car on a snow-packed road and wait for another car to creep along at about five miles per hour. Just as it was passing, he'd jump out and grab hold of the moving car's rear bumper and slide along behind it. Not too bright, right? Still, it's a perfect illustration of what music can do. Catchy melodies have a way of grabbing hold of our subconscious and hitching a ride. They can sneak up from behind and hook on without much warning. We have to shake them loose. Or better yet, keep our eyes open so they don't latch on in the first place.

Billboard magazine ran a guest commentary by Dr. Richard Pellegrino, a brain specialist with a fascinating take on the power of music. He talked about potent chemical reactions in the brain. He explained how music can actually improve visual and spatial reasoning, memory, and learning. After discussing "music's immense power" and urging artists and producers to use that power wisely, Dr. Pellegrino concluded, "Take it from a brain guy: In 25 years of working with the human brain, I still cannot affect a person's state of mind the way that one simple song can." Now *that's* powerful!

! cause and effect

"We've put out songs with lyrics in them that we thought people would think were funny, but they ended up having a lot of really negative effects on people. [Performers] need to be aware that when you're creating music it has a tremendous influence on society."

—Adam Youch of Beastie Boys

explicit stuff

Lyrics about sex and drugs aren't new. Sure, they've gotten bolder since your parents were in high school, but even back then some music strayed out of bounds. In the late 1970s, Eric Clapton had a hit single titled "Cocaine." And while oldies might not use graphic sexual slang, songs like Billy Joel's "Only the Good Die Young" and Meat Loaf's "Paradise by the Dashboard Light" still had their hormones in overdrive.

Joel now admits that people who raised concerns about early rock music had a valid point. "All those things they were saying about rock 'n' roll in the early days—'Oh, it's gonna subvert our youth. It's gonna make 'em all want to have sex. It's gonna make 'em all go crazy'—they were *right*." Quite a confession. Today, chart-topping lyrics continue to get more and more explicit, making the need for discernment even more crucial.

Music is a mighty motivator, even when it's not trying to be. Def Jam Records founder Russel Simmons was quite proud when Jay-Z's casual reference to a clothing company inspired a run on designer sweaters. "Jay-Z raps about Iceberg and it catches fire," Simmons boasted. "That's a fact. The minute he said it, Saks Fifth Avenue blows out Iceberg sweaters at what?—$600 apiece. Instantly!" And what of Jay-Z's lyrics that make illicit sex, gang violence, and drunk driving look cool? Are we to believe they have absolutely no impact whatsoever? If they're honest, even the artists don't really believe that.

It seems more and more musicians are rethinking choices they've made. That includes goth rocker Trent Reznor of Nine Inch Nails, who said, "I think *The Downward Spiral* actually could be harmful through implying and subliminally suggesting things."

Power to Control?

"Music is such a powerful medium now. The kids don't even know who the president is, but they know what's on MTV. I think if anyone like Hitler or Mussolini were alive now, they would have to be rock stars."

—Marilyn Manson

perform surgery ▌▎▎▎ ▎▎ ▎

Okay, so the messages in songs have a powerful impact. Now what? How can a young man of God be discerning and defend himself against audio trash? Dissect and discard.

It's a lot like that biology class where you have to cut up a frog. You take your spiritual scalpel and rip into a song to take a closer look at its guts. What do the lyrics really say? Of course, when you dissect a frog, you have a chart or diagram that tells you what to look for and what function each organ serves. When dissecting a song, you can use the truth of Scripture as a guide to know what you're dealing with. Does a disc include profanity? Well, Proverbs 4:24 says:

> Put away perversity from your mouth;
> keep corrupt talk far from your lips.

Does it present violent, promiscuous, pot-smoking thugs as attractive role models? Proverbs 24:1 warns:

> Do not envy wicked men,
> do not desire their company.

Does it advocate hatred or disrespect toward Mom and Dad? Exodus 20:12 tells us to *honor* our parents.

More than a scalpel, the Word of God is a double-edged sword (Hebrews 4:12) with an answer for everything. Those verses and others will help you skillfully dissect song lyrics. Then, once you've ripped them open, it's time to discard anything that contradicts God's healthy plan for your life. It's never easy to say *adiós* to favorite CDs that don't make the cut. Just keep in mind that purifying your music library is essential if you're serious about achieving personal holiness. Check out this statement by Louie Giglio, founder of the Passion worship movement. It really sums up how we should think of music:

> I think all music—not just Christian music but all music—is worship music because every song is amplifying the value of something. . . . There's a trail of our time, our affection, our allegiance, our devotion, our money. That trail leads to a throne, and whatever's on that throne is what we worship.

So, what are you worshipping?

"I've had every video game system there is. It's a trap once you get involved with that stuff. It becomes like this drug in a weird way."

—Actor Leonardo DiCaprio

The days of Pong and Pac Man are over. Space Invaders is history. Today's interactive video games are faster, more realistic, and—some people would argue—more addictive.

Just how popular are console and CD-ROM games? By the late 1990s, video game sales accounted for more than $6 billion per year. That's more than double the figure for 1995!

Stats also suggest that it's definitely a guy thing. Only 31 percent of girls age 13 to 17 play video games at home, while a whopping 63 percent of guys do. And why not? Guys love a good adrenaline rush. After all, it's one thing to watch an action movie, but with advanced video game technology, you can feel like you're in an action movie. Awesome! And you're totally in control . . . or are you?

the truth about VIOLENT VIDEO games

After a series of school shootings, violent video games drew special attention. Authorities found that the shooters, almost without exception, were big fans of point-and-shoot games. That sparked debate over the games' ability to fuel real-life hostility. Recent research shows that playing violent games *can* increase aggressive thoughts, feelings, and behavior. Does that mean every guy who plays Duke Nukem will turn into a cold-blooded killer? No way. That's unrealistic. But it would be equally foolish to pretend that there's no risk from games that stimulate endorphins, encourage brutality, and then *reward* violence—a potent combination.

Are violent video games dangerous? Lt. Col. David Grossman, director of the Killology Research Group, is an expert on what it takes to make soldiers more comfortable with taking another life on the battlefield. He sees a parallel with games that put players behind the eyes of the shooter. Just as a flight simulator teaches people to fly a plane, so point-and-shoot games can desensitize us and, in extreme cases, make people more efficient killers.

"In Paducah, Ky., a 14-year-old boy brought a .22 caliber pistol to school," Lt. Col. Grossman explains. "He fired eight shots. For the sake of perspective, the FBI says that the average law enforcement officer hits less than one bullet in five in real-world engagement. This young man fired eight shots. He hit eight different students. And we know where he acquired this ability—from video games. His parents had converted a two-car garage into a playroom with VCRs and video games. He had become a master game player.

"On that fateful morning, he acted out a set of conditioned responses. He walked in, planted his feet, posted the gun in a two-handed stance, and opened fire. He never moved far to the left or right. He just fired one shot at everything that popped up on his screen. A person's normal response is to shoot at a target until it drops, but video games train you to fire one shot and then move on. And so he proceeded. Most video games give bonus points for head shots. This young man hit five out of eight in that region."

Creepy. And tragic. Of course, few players will take gaming to that extreme, but a man of God shouldn't entertain himself with violence in the first place. Even if you'd never kill someone, could you be nurturing a love for violence?

WHAT DOES GOD SAY?

"The LORD examines the righteous,
but the wicked and those who love violence
his soul hates."

—Psalm 11:5

the DESENSITIZING EFFECT

For the rare guy who plays Quake or Grand Theft Auto 3 and goes postal, there are countless others who never get that close to the edge and yet are still being desensitized to pain and suffering. Brutal video games aren't the only culprits (though, being interactive, they can co-opt emotions in a powerful way). Toss in graphic images of car bombings on the nightly news. Add TV shows replaying real-life crime or tragic accidents. Factor in guys like Johnny Knoxville. What you get is a visceral smorgasbord without any moral context. A steady diet of that kind of media is what causes people to slow down and gawk at car wrecks instead of being horrified by them. We get a little too used to violence. Before you know it, the line between pixellated figures on the screen and real people starts to get blurry, and the Christlike compassion that should flow out of us has slowed to a trickle.

MORE STUFF TO THINK ABOUT

Before you invest time, money, and energy in a video game, break it down and discern what persona it's asking you to put on. Are you playing the kind of hero who reflects godly character? Or is the game leading you to make poor moral choices in the name of fantasy? Here's what the average joystick jockey runs into:

Self-centeredness. When you are self-centered, you believe that you are the center of the universe. No one else matters. Your goals must be achieved and your desires satisfied, even if that means breaking rules or hurting others. Sounds like most of the game characters out there, doesn't it? Wipe out people and property to score points. Crush! Kill! Destroy! And you're rewarded for it!

Violent problem solving. Ecclesiastes 9:18 tells us, "Wisdom is better than weapons of war." Try telling that to the creators of today's best-selling titles. To make it through various levels, you're armed with everything from handguns to automatic weapons to bazookas to smart bombs. You put your faith in firepower.

Materialism. This is the belief that "things" can satisfy our deepest needs. The meaning of life lies in obtaining more stuff. Many games set players on a quest for wealth, a chunk of real estate, or some special artifact. The hero is ultimately successful not because he has grown in character but because he *acquires* something.

Relativism. The belief that there are no moral absolutes or eternal principles is called relativism. No right or wrong. You decide at any given moment what is appropriate. Some video games may not include random violence or sexual content, yet they still ask you to play the part of a character who lies, steals, or makes other fundamentally immoral choices to accomplish a noble goal. Should we be training our minds to deceive?

Occultism. In occultism, one places reliance on ungodly supernatural powers, believing that they can be controlled for human use. Games often portray the legions of darkness as the potent supernatural force, trivializing God or leaving Him out of the equation altogether. Typically, players have little choice except to fight evil with evil (spells, sorcery, etc.) or storm the gates of hell with guns a-blazin'.

MODERATION IS THE KEY

In 2 John 10-11, we're told, "If anyone comes to you and does not bring [God's] teaching, do not take him into your house or welcome him. Anyone who welcomes him shares in his wicked work." So, why do we invite video games into our homes and onto our hard drives when these games are excessively violent or reflect philosophies that directly contradict our Christian faith?

Remember, computer games are not inherently evil. There are some great ones out there that, played in moderation, can be a lot of fun. If you're having a tough time figuring out where to draw the line, pray about it. James 1:5 promises, "If any of you lacks wisdom, he should ask God, who gives generously to all without finding fault, and it will be given to him." Come to think of it, being transformed into the image of Jesus Christ is kinda like playing a video game: We're always trying to reach the next level!

CHAPTER EIGHTEEN: TV AND MOVIES: HOW TO AVOID MIND MELTDOWN

"Film is a powerful medium. Film is a drug. Film is a potential hallucinogen. It goes into your eye. It goes into your brain. It stimulates. And it's a dangerous thing. It can be a very subversive thing."

—Oliver Stone, director of *Platoon*, *JFK*, and *Natural Born Killers*

Scene One: Movie Magic—or Madness? A dark theater. Reclining seats. Surround sound. Hot-buttered popcorn. There's something almost magical about seeing a movie on the big screen. Add friends and a cold drink to the mix, and you've got the makings of a perfect afternoon, right? Not so fast. There's more to a motion picture than cool special effects and a rip-roaring soundtrack. The images and messages contained in films can leave a permanent mark on our attitudes—whether we want them to or not.

"Two girls came up to me and said they'd changed their names on their birth certificates to Sarah, so they could be just like my character on Party of Five."

—Jennifer Love Hewitt

Scene Two: Tube Tales. Until 1995, the residents of Fiji couldn't watch television. It simply didn't exist there. Immediately after it was introduced, the islanders noticed a sharp rise in eating disorders. Then, just three years after TV flickered into their lives, 74 percent of girls said they felt "too big or too fat."

"Nobody was dieting in Fiji ten years ago," reports Harvard Medical School anthropology professor Anne Becker. *"The teenagers see TV as a model for how one gets by in the modern world. They believe the shows depict reality."*

Is it really much different in North America? From fashions to hairstyles, we take many of our cues from what we see on the big screen or on the tube. Our sense of reality is shaped by it. And it's not just the way we look. Often it's the way we talk. The way we think. The way we act.

Let's zoom in for a closer look at movies and TV. While we're at it, we'll dissect our viewing habits and see if we can find a better way to be entertained.

MOVIES: DON'T CHECK YOUR BRAIN AT THE DOOR

Movies featuring explicit sex, violence, language, or occultism are no-brainers. They're clearly out of bounds based on verses such as Psalm 101:3, Philippians 4:8, Colossians 2:8, and 1 John 2:15-17. However, some movies can be a lot of fun! The important thing is that you don't leave your brain in the lobby after the dude with the name tag tears your ticket. Here are just a few questions to ask as you watch movies:

What's the point? Boiled down to its most basic theme, what is the flick trying to say?

Which characters am I being asked to root for? Are they virtuous people, or am I supposed to find immorality heroic?

Are the characters thinking about the long-term consequences of their decisions? If I went out and did the stuff the people on-screen are doing, what would probably happen in the real world?

What is the filmmaker trying to get me to think or feel? If I went along with it, would that enrich my spiritual life, or could it drag me down?

What is the "power source"? Where do the characters find strength and answers to their problems? Is it in God and eternal truth, or do they rely on human wisdom or the occult to deal with conflict? What does the story say about God?

Heroes or Villains?

"Half the business called Hollywood is sleaze. A lot of what we do has very little to do with art. It has to do with sleaze and gratuitous sex and unnecessary violence."

—Film and television actor Martin Sheen

Have you ever been sitting there in a theater, munching your Raisinettes, when out of nowhere came an explicit sex scene, some brutal violence, or a really raunchy joke? What did you do? Most guys would brush it off and keep watching. After all, who drops 10 bucks on admission and snacks and then walks out after only 15 minutes? Frankly, a man of God does!

The Lord cares deeply about the stuff we put into our systems. If we're serious about following Him, we need to be more concerned about our spiritual fitness than about how much money we spent or what our friends might think. (By the way, most theater managers will give you a refund or a comp ticket if you bag on a film because of offensive content.)

Teens who have taken that kind of stand are leaders. They're bold. They want to do what's right regardless of the cost. Romans 12:1 says we must present ourselves to God as a living and holy sacrifice.

There's a cost involved in that. If you go out and buy designer clothes, you pay a price to wear that designer's name. On your chest. On your back pocket. On your hat. On your shoes. The cost depends on the designer. Well, if you want to bear the name of Jesus, there's a similar cost involved. But it's not a one-time charge of $70 for a pair of jeans or $40 for a shirt. It's a price we pay every day in the choices we make.

KNOW BEFORE YOU GO

If you don't like the idea of walking out on a movie (who does?), there are ways to avoid getting into that situation in the first place. Learn as much as you can about a movie *before* heading to the local cineplex. Web sites like pluggedinmag.com or previewonline.org can give you the scoop on new movies from a Christian perspective so you'll know what's in store. If, after doing a little research, you and your parents agree that it's an okay flick, go for it! If you see something that you don't believe God would consider appropriate, listen to the Holy Spirit and find something else.

Sometimes it's real tempting to go along with the crowd when a bunch of friends are dead set on checking out a certain film. They're psyched to see the latest horror film or teen sex comedy. Yet you know it's not right. What do you do? Without being judgmental, let them know you'd rather not see the movie but that you'd like to meet up with them afterward if they're going out for burgers or pizza. This reinforces that you're most interested in spending time with your friends—not sitting in a dark theater where you can't even talk to each other. Chances are, they'll respect that.

WHAT ABOUT R-RATED MOVIES?

A *Breakaway* reader once asked the question "Can I watch an R-rated movie and still be a Christian?" Let's look closely at that one.

First things first. The question reveals a fundamental misunderstanding of what it really means to be a Christian. Our salvation has nothing to do with entertainment. It comes as a result of what Jesus did on the cross. He died as a sacrifice for our sin, earning us the right to share a relationship with God now and spend eternity with Him in heaven after we die. It's a gift. We simply need to accept it by faith.

So if we ask, "Can I watch an R-rated movie and still be a Christian?" we're making two false assumptions. The first is that going to a movie can somehow undo what Jesus did at Calvary. Make no mistake: Watching an R-rated film (or a lot of PG-13 releases for that matter) *can* hurt our spiritual growth, but they can't rob us of our salvation.

The second false assumption is that our relationship with God is based on works—a perfect performance. In other words, if we avoid the bad stuff, we maintain our Christian status. Well, that's misleading too. Remember, you bear the name "Christian" because of what Jesus did.

Yes, we should avoid entertainment that God would disapprove of. And R-rated movies, by definition, warn us that they include some pretty edgy stuff. But you shouldn't skip a raunchy comedy or gory slasher pic out of fear that if you see them you'll lose your place in heaven. Rather, skip 'em in response to what Jesus did on the cross and out of love for Him. He paid the price. If you really intend to serve Him—and want His best for your life—you should honor Christ in everything you do. That includes the movies you check out, both at the theater and on video.

tv: WHat's WITH tHe tube?

It's kind of funny when you stop to think about it. The same average Joes who say television has no power at all will go to wild extremes to be seen on it. They appear on humiliating talk shows like Jerry Springer and risk embarrassment on reality series like *Survivor* or *Fear Factor*. From Johnny Knoxville to advertisers to those guys at ball games who hold up signs saying "SportsCenter Is Next," everyone knows that TV gets seen and has the ability to impact viewers.

! Fact or Fiction?

"When we first started, all our technical advisers told us that emergency rooms were the primary source of health care for most Americans. That's changed in recent years, because watching *ER* has become the primary source of health information. Then people go to the emergency room and compare."

—Noah Wyle of the popular NBC drama *ER*

DON'T LET TV SKEW YOUR VIEW

Television sends out a constant stream of messages on what seem like 40 million channels. An awful lot of those messages sell you and your friends a bad bill of goods in (among other things) the area of sexuality. Racy advertising. Immodest music videos. Scandalous news items. And what about sitcoms, dramas, and reality shows that make sex outside of marriage—even homosexuality—seem normal and healthy?

A while back, *YM* magazine published the results of an on-line poll of nearly 15,000 teenage girls. It asked them why they were choosing to have sex. As it turned out, the number-one reason girls decided to become sexually active was *curiosity*. More than half (58 percent) said they gave away the most intimate gift ever just because they wanted to know what all the fuss was about. While this survey was of young women, it's safe to say that a lot of guys venture into that territory for pretty much the same reason.

What fuels that kind of curiosity? The media, for one. Sitcom humor is *obsessed* with sex. Dramas often use sexuality to spice up subplots. A year-long study of the WWF's "Raw Is War" by folks at Indiana University found 128 simulated sex acts in and around the ring. And MTV? Fuggeddaboudit! With sex getting so much attention on the tube, is it any wonder teens wanna know whassup?

take every thought captive

The prevalence of sexual themes can be tough for us guys. After all, we're wired for visual stimulation. Lust is a constant enemy.

Just ask King David. His eyes got him into trouble. He wasn't tuned in to *Baywatch* or *MTV's Undressed*. He wasn't watching *Sports Illustrated* swimsuit models on pay cable. He was simply observing a woman bathing. But the effect was the same. It started a fire inside of him that resulted in devastating consequences. That's why David's words in Psalm 101:3—"I will set before my eyes no vile thing"—carry so much weight. He's not saying that attractive women are vile. But he is saying, "Ultimately, I'm in charge of what I put into my system, and I'm not going to expose myself to anything that could lead me to sin."

In the New Testament, the apostle Paul put it another way. Despite never getting HBO or the Playboy Channel, he knew how effectively Satan uses our idle thoughts against us. That's why Paul warned the Corinthian church, "Take captive every thought to make it obedient to Christ" (2 Corinthians 10:5). Think of that next time you're surfing with the remote. For the serious-minded man of God, there's no such thing as vegging out with mindless TV. Stay sharp.

! taking back control

"You can bury my TV. There's nothing to watch—just bad things and naked people."

—Quote from an elderly Moscow woman after an antenna fire disrupted TV broadcasting there.

KEEP YOUR **BRAIN ENGAGED** ▮▮▮▮ ▮▮ ▮ ▮

Soaking up sexual images and philosophies is just one prime-time hazard for guys. There are others. Some shows can inspire an unhealthy fascination with the occult. Some rely heavily on violence. The point is, TV shows reflect the worldviews of the people making them. And it's rarely a biblical worldview!

When you stop to consider that each year the average guy spends 900 hours in school and nearly 1,500 hours watching TV, you've gotta wonder where he's doing most of his "learning." A man of God has to keep his brain engaged at all times. Here are some things to think about:

In a sitcom, problems are introduced and solved in a 30-minute period. As you may have noticed, real life rarely works out that way.

When you see a scene of violence or emotional cruelty on a show or in a commercial, is the perpetrator punished? Are you led to empathize with the victims' suffering, or is their pain simply meant to entertain you? Avoid being desensitized.

On television, there's a great deal of emphasis on people's looks. Buff bod. Perfect hair. Pearly white grin. Remember the words of 1 Samuel 16:7: "The LORD does not look at the things man looks at. Man looks at the outward appearance, but the LORD looks at the heart."

TV often relies on stereotypes. For example, in a 30-minute show, it's faster and easier to portray a "nerdy guy" by giving him Coke-bottle glasses taped in the middle than by developing him as a human being. Don't let these shortcuts affect the way you view people.

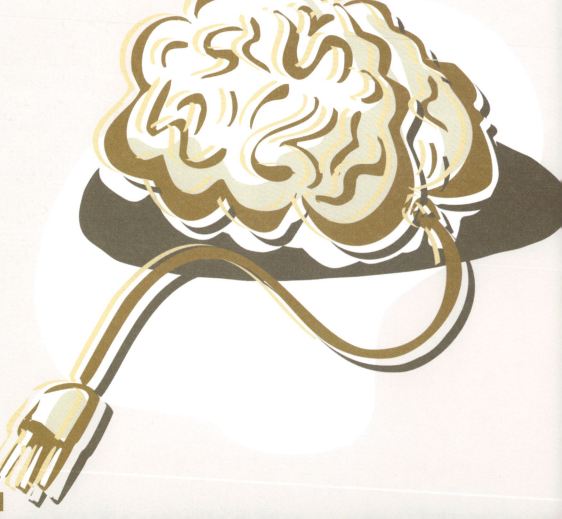

Plan your viewing ahead of time. It's easy to channel-surf an afternoon away without ever resting on a show for more than five minutes at a time. Budget a reasonable amount of time each week for the tube. Then grab a highlighter and the *TV Guide* and make some wise choices.

Sometimes the best course of action is to turn off the set. Prime-time companionship can't compare to hours spent with godly friends. The apostle Paul told young Timothy, "Flee the evil desires of youth, and pursue righteousness, faith, love and peace, along with those who call on the Lord out of a pure heart" (2 Timothy 2:22).

CHAPTER NINETEEN: a WEB OF CHOICES | | | || | |

So you like sailing through cyberspace? Saving the planet from rogue aliens? Editing your own movies? Computer technology moves faster all the time, but if anybody moves just as fast, it's teen guys. Can you even remember when there wasn't an Internet?

Yet, as with other aspects of life, the virtual world has a good side and a dark side. Many guys are using the Web for positive—even eternal—purposes. Unfortunately, some guys (not to mention thousands of other teens and adults—even Breakaway readers) are tuning in to the bad stuff, too.

Take a look:

THE GOOD SIDE | | | || || | |

Bulletin boards. Chat rooms. Photo galleries. Video viewing rooms. Music downloads. Encyclopedias. Whole libraries. There are plenty of good reasons to cruise cyberspace. Log on to the Web, click the mouse, and you're walking the halls of the U.S. Capitol. Click again, and you're face-to-face with a pride of lions on an African safari. *Click.* A NASA Web page—with tons of information that'll help you with your big report. *Click.* A Bible story. *Click.* Encode. *Click.* You can create a home page for your own youth group.

ninety-four percent

Ninety-four percent of on-line teens report researching on the Internet for school projects.

THE DARK SIDE ▮▮▮▮▮▮▮ ▮

Click. Anarchist ideologies. *Click.* Drug connections. *Click.* The occult. *Click.* Sexual predators. *Click.* Digital piracy. *Click. Click. Click.* You started in your best friend's video game review site and within a few quick clicks ended up in archives of hard-core pornography. *Click.* Gambling galore and big-time financial ruin.

! NEARLY SIXTY PERCENT

Nearly sixty percent of teens have received an IM (instant message) or e-mail from a stranger.

THE DILEMMA ▮▮▮▮▮▮ ▮

Our technologically driven society *demands* a working knowledge of "virtual" interaction. Many parts of the academic and business worlds are totally dependent on this far-reaching technology for research, information, and countless other activities. Thousands trade stocks and bank on-line. Public libraries, churches, and schools have launched Web sites. And

! FIFTEEN PERCENT

Fifteen percent of on-line teens and 25 percent of older boys on-line have lied about their age to access a Web site—an act often used to enter a pornographic site.

Christian ministries that spread the gospel get a lot of help from the mass communication inherent to the Internet.

Obviously, pulling the plug on cyberspace isn't so easy in this day and age. So, what's a *Breakaway* guy to do? How can you tune in the good stuff and avoid the bad?

seventy-three percent

About 17 million teens and tweens ages 12 to 17 use the Internet, according to recent research conducted by the Pew Internet & American Life Project. That's 73 percent of youth in that age bracket.

navigating THE NET ▌▌▌ ▌ ▌ ▌▌ ▌

It all begins with a pretty simple, time-honored concept—watch where you wander. Or in this case, watch where you click your mouse.

The Web is like a big city, an amazing megalopolis of cybercircuitry with wide boulevards and narrow alleys, churches and nightclubs. It also contains a gushing cybersewer and a blazing red-light district of sleazy bookstores and smut shops. But remember, when Jesus promised His assistance and companionship "to the very end of the age" (Matthew 28:20), He *already* knew all about the Internet. His power and friendship stretch into cyberspace, too!

YES, YOU CAN

Okay, we know what you're thinking: *The temptation is just too much to handle. When it comes to cyberporn and the other dark sides of the Net, it's so easy to give in . . . and hard to get out.*

True. But teen guys can get out—and STAY OUT—of that vast emptiness of digitized danger that's just a click away. Cruising safely down the information superhighway is possible. You've just got to use some biblical standards and old-fashioned common sense.

Seventy percent of on-line families have their Internet-connected computer located in an open area of the house such as a den.

cyberspace survival tips

Cut off the source. Many filtering software packages block sexually explicit material before it gets to your screen. Get one.

Don't surf alone. Stay off the Web when you're home alone. Secrecy only adds to the temptation. Stick to wide open spaces. Keep the computer out of your bedroom and in a common area, like the kitchen or den, where you know a family member could walk by at any minute.

Keep accountable. Talk with a close friend, youth pastor, even a parent. They can pray, encourage you, and help monitor your time on-line. Plus, knowing they're going to ask you about your latest cyber-session will make you think twice before clicking on that graphic game or swimsuit model.

Study history. No, not the kind in school—your computer's log of where you've been on the Web. Let your accountability partner—or your parents—browse through your records. What have you got to hide?

Invite Mom or Dad along for the ride. If you're really serious, bring 'em along to your favorite sites and show Mom and Dad what you do in cyberspace. Don't use the computer after the rest of your family is in bed. Just like city streets, the Internet (especially chat rooms) is more hazardous when traversed in the dark.

Be street-smart. This is especially true in cyberspace: Don't talk to strangers.

Guard your family's privacy. Never give out your name, address, phone number, or any other personal information on the Web.

Don't chat alone. IM a friend and take him along. You can carry on your own conversations but know that a buddy can back you up—and keep you from posing as that 25-year-old bodybuilding, Ferrari-driving secret agent.

Leave chat rooms immediately if anyone pressures you to talk, harasses you in any way, or asks for personal information. Never respond to suggestive, belligerent, sexual, abusive, or degrading messages. Always let your service provider know if these things happen to you.

Never go alone to meet anyone face-to-face. If you do discover someone on the Net whom you want to meet in the real world, make sure your parents are with you and make sure the meeting happens in a public place.

Never play with pornographic sites. Satan will try to tell you otherwise, especially in the heat of the moment, but such sites are dangerous to your soul and your future marriage. For the same reason you would never play with matches in a closet, you should never, ever visit sordid Web sites.

Trust your conscience. Feeling a little uneasy about what's flashing on your screen? *But those women aren't naked; they've got a few strings on.* Wouldn't want your mom to walk in right now? *Okay, so I lied about my age and bet $10, but it's just a game.* Yeah, you know the feeling. That's the Holy Spirit letting you know what Jesus would do: get out of there. Quit the rationalizing, and get out quick.

Memorize Scripture. Check out Psalm 101:3, 2 Corinthians 10:5, Philippians 4:8, and 2 Timothy 2:22. Print 'em out, and stick 'em on your monitor as a constant reminder.

IM mania

Seventy-four percent of on-line teens use instant messaging (IM). That's close to 13 million teens.

Seventeen percent of IM users have used IM to ask someone out. Thirteen percent have used it to break up.

Nineteen percent of on-line teens say they use IM most often to contact their friends when they are not with them. Seventy-one percent still use the telephone.

Twenty-four percent of on-line teens have created their own Web pages.

get a REAL LIFE ▮ ▮ ▮ ▮ ▮▮ ▮ ▮

Find that you're going by your nick more than your real name? Are all your friends on-line? Having to use drops to clear your bloodshot eyes because you've been staring at the screen too long? Are you impatient all day at school to get back to cyberspace? Maybe it's time to log off—for a while.

As cool as it can be, the Web can't replace real life. You need real contact with real people to keep you in touch with reality. But it's easy to surf the day away on-line, often without even realizing it.

To avoid getting sucked in:

Set time limits. Set an alarm to go off after a predetermined period.

Turn off. When time is up, shut down your system.

Listen to your mother or father. When your parents ask you to log off, do it.

Get social. Do at least one non-computer-related social activity a week with real people. Go to youth group or play Frisbee in the yard. Shopping for software doesn't count.

DOWNLOAD THIS! (WORTHY WEB SITES)

Breakaway (www.BreakawayMag.com). Duh! Get what's in print plus more.

Plugged In (www.pluggedinmag.com). Focus on the Family's music and movie reviews.

"Life on the Edge Live!" (www.family.org/lotelive). Focus on the Family's live talk radio show for teens—starring you.

Boundless (www.boundless.org). Focus on the Family's Webzine for college students.

Christian Teens (http://christianteens.about.com). Info and links on issues, faith, missions, and more.

Encarta (http://encarta.msn.com). On-line encyclopedia includes homework help.

Encyclopedia.com (www.encyclopedia.com). Just like it says.

Christian Students (www.christianstudents.com). Tons of links to teen issues and topics.

Made 4 More (www.made4more.com). Questions and answers about life, sex, and hope.

Musicforce.com (www.musicforce.com). The latest Christian CDs.

Peterson's (www.petersons.com). Comprehensive guide to colleges, career planning, even summer camps and programs.

Reference: Best Source for Facts on the Net (www.refdesk.com). You name it, this site's got it: facts, info, trivia, news, maps, etc.

See You at the Pole (www.syatp.com). All about the event, the ministry, and more.

CCM Magazine (www.ccmmagazine.com). The latest on and inside Christian music.

Sports Spectrum (www.sport.org). Christian sports magazine.

WHAT'S UP ON-LINE

The percentage of teens with Internet access who have done the following activities on-line:

Sent or read e-mail—92%

Surfed the Web for fun—84%

Visited an entertainment site—83%

Sent an instant message—74%

Looked for info on hobbies—69%

Got news—68%

Played or downloaded a game—66%

Researched a product or service before buying it—66%

Received e-mail or instant messages from a stranger—60%

Listened to music on-line—59%

Visited a chat room—55%

Exchanged e-mail or instant messages with strangers—50%

Shared passwords—22%

Lied about their age to access a Web site—15%

Sent a prank e-mail—6%

Aluminum Records (www.aluminumrecords.com)

Ardent Records (www.ArdentRecords.com)

BEC Recordings (www.BECrecordings.com)

Essential Records (www.EssentialRecords.com)

Fervent Records (www.FerventRecords.com)

5 Minute Walk Records (www.5MinuteWalk.com)

FlickerRecords.com (www.FlickerRecords.com)

Forefront Records (www.ForefrontRecords.com)

40 Records (www.40Records.com)

Gotee Records (www.Gotee.com)

Grapetree Records (www.GrapetreeRecords.com)

Inotof Records (www.Inotof.com)

Inpop Records (www.Inpop.com)

Integrity Music (www.IntegrityMusic.com)

Lion of Zion Entertainment (www.LionofZion.com)

Metro 1 Music (www.Metro1Music.com)

Organic Records (www.OrganicRecords.com)

Pamplin Music (www.PamplinMusic.com)

Reunion Records (www.ReunionRecords.com)

Rhythm House Records (www.RhythmHouse.com)

Rocketown Records (www.RocketownRecords.com)

Rustproof Records (www.rustproofrecords.com)

Silent Planet Records (www.SilentPlanetRecords.com)

Solid State Records (www.SolidStateRecords.com)

Sparrow Records (www.SparrowRecords.com)

Squint Entertainment (www.Squinterland.com)

Tooth & Nail Records (www.ToothandNail.com)

Uprok Records (www.UprokRecords.com)

Verity Records (www.verityrecordsonline.com)

Watershed Records (www.WatershedRecords.com)

Word Records (www.WordRecords.com)

PART SIX: WHO WANTS TO BE a teenage MILLIONAIRE

CHAPTER TWENTY: MONEY—WHAT THE BIBLE SAYS

Pick up any dictionary, and it might define success as something like this: "the setting and then achieving of one's goals." In other words, a person decides what he wants and then works hard until he reaches that goal. That's what a success is. But what does it mean to be successful?

You could say that a person who has lots of success, one who sets lots of goals and then continually achieves them, would be successful. But that's not exactly what most people think about when they think of being successful.

If a person is considered successful, he's probably at the top of his career. Who's topping the music charts right now? That person or group is probably a success in your book. And what about the movies? Who's the best actor out there, pulling down the top salary and starring in the best movies? To you, that guy is probably a success.

When it comes to sports, can anyone dispute that Kobe Bryant rules the court? And Tiger Woods is unquestionably the king of the fairways. Both of these guys are leaders in their sports. When you see them in the news, is there any doubt in your mind that they are successful?

At this point in your life, you probably haven't narrowed down exactly what you will do for a living when you become an adult. However, no matter what that career might end up being, if you become the number-one person in that career, will you be considered successful?

Maybe, but not always.

SUCCESS IN GOD'S EYES

It's important to understand that God sees success differently than the world does. He doesn't look at how great of a sports star a person is or how much money he brings home from commercial endorsements. God doesn't care what kind of car a person drives, how big his house is, or even if he owns a platinum credit card with no spending limit. All the power, money, and fame in the world don't impress God the least bit, because He doesn't define success in the same way the world does.

Then how, exactly, *does* God define success? To begin understanding the answer to that question, look at this list of biblical characters who were successful in God's eyes:

Abraham—When he was as old as your grandfather, he had his first child and became the father of an entire nation. God honored Abraham's faith by working miracles in his life despite his old age.

Joseph—As a teen, he dreamed of becoming the ruler of a nation. Joseph was sold into slavery by his own brothers and spent years rotting in a jail. But because of Joseph's faith, God moved him from the dungeon to Egypt's governor's palace overnight!

! SUCCESS STATISTICS

According to Barna Research:

- Fifty-one percent of Christians and 54 percent of non-Christians believe that money is the main symbol of success in life.

- Thirty-two percent of Christians and 44 percent of non-Christians say money is very important to them.

- Nineteen percent of Christians and 20 percent of non-Christians think you can tell how successful someone is by looking at what they own.

- **David**—As a young shepherd and the least member of his family, David tended the family's flocks, fighting off bears and lions in hand-to-hand combat. While he watched the sheep, he developed a passionate faith in the Almighty Creator. As a result, God made David the king of Israel!

- **Peter**—He started life as the son of a fisherman. Somewhere down the line, he met Jesus and became a disciple of Christ. As he followed Jesus, he developed an unshakable faith. God made him the first leader of Christianity, building the early Church through Peter's leadership.

- **Paul**—When the Christian Church first started, Paul (who was at that time named Saul) made it his mission in life to destroy the movement before it could take root. During a trip to Damascus, Jesus appeared to him and changed his life forever. Paul became the Church's first missionary, and God used Paul's granitelike faith to provide wisdom and guidance to the Body of Christ all over the world. He ended up writing about half the New Testament!

When we look at this list, we see that the common denominator is faith. These men all had a deep, unshakable, loving, and transforming faith in God. A faith like that doesn't happen overnight. It comes as a result of building a powerful relationship with God over a long period of time.

Success in God's eyes has nothing to do with how *much* you can do or make or achieve. In God's sight, success has everything to do with how much we love Him and desire to serve Him, no matter the cost. When a person has that, there's nothing that will keep him from being a success in God's eyes.

a guy with a faith leading to godly success . . .

. . . never says, "God, this is what *I* want." Instead, he always asks, "God what do *You* want?"

. . . never says, "God, I *won't* . . ." Instead, he always says, "God, I'll do Your will."

. . . never looks for self-satisfaction. Instead, he looks to satisfy God.

. . . never seeks mankind's approval. Instead, he seeks God's approval.

. . . never measures success by how well things are going. Instead, he measures success by a life centered in God's will.

. . . never puts his needs first. Instead, he always thinks of others first.

. . . never looks to his own capabilities to solve a problem. Instead, he relies fully on God's power to lead him.

Success in God's eyes runs counter to what the world says success is. Success in God's eyes means a person must be willing to give up everything—himself, his possessions, his pride, his power—in order to gain what God has in store for him. It's sometimes true that in doing so a guy may never achieve what he dreamed he'd always become. However, when a guy fully surrenders his life, God often returns those dreams and talents. But one thing is always true: God's plans for you are bigger, grander, and more wild than you could ever imagine.

Bottom line, if a guy wants to become a success in God's eyes, he chooses to surrender everything to God and to God's will for his life. When a guy reaches this level of relationship with the Father, there's little doubt that he will become a success in God's eyes.

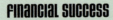

financial success

So, are you fully surrendered to God? Are you totally trusting in God to provide your needs on a daily basis? Not sure?

What about your finances? Does God have control of your finances, too? Are you tithing on every penny you make? God asks His people to give back to Him from what He has blessed them with. If you're not giving at least your tithe to God, then you're not totally surrendered to Him.

That's a pretty harsh statement. Some people would even disagree with that statement, saying that tithing was only an Old Testament principle. As the Christian Church is "no longer under the law, but under grace," these people say Christians don't have to tithe.

But if that were so, why did Abraham tithe more than 400 years before the law was written? He didn't have the law, and he still tithed. And nowhere in the New Testament does it say that Christians don't have to or shouldn't tithe. Therefore, it's a fair bet that tithing is still a valid principle for Christians to live by.

give your 10 percent

Tithe is an Old English word that simply means "tenth." God asks His people to return to Him 10 percent of the wealth He blesses them with. In return, God promises to pour out blessings on those who tithe. God actually challenges His people to see if He won't bless them incredibly as they tithe (Malachi 3:10).

In Malachi 3, God has stiff words regarding tithing. He says that people who won't return to Him at least 10 percent of what He's blessed them with are robbing Him. God also says He withholds blessings from those who will not tithe.

In our market-driven society, one of the most difficult areas to put under God's control is our money. Having total control of one's financial matters is one way to demonstrate a person's success to the world. That's one reason why people have such a difficult time giving God control of their finances. Also, since there's not always a visible return on financial investment in God's kingdom, this is another reason why people find it hard to tithe. They just don't see the point.

If you're going to get on God's pathway to success, your finances will have to come under God's total control. God wants you to trust Him on this. He wants to prove to you that He's not going to let you go broke. In fact, if you trust Him completely in this area, He's promised to flood your life with uncountable blessings.

tithe your time | | | | | | | | |

Okay, we've discussed tithing your money, but what about your time? You go to church every Sunday. You attend youth group meetings on a regular basis. You participate in the activities the youth group does. You even tithe your money. Isn't that enough? What else could God want?

Though the Bible never actually says it, tithing your time is a good idea too. That means setting aside at least 10 percent of your time for God's work. It's important to understand, however, that this tithe does not include the time you spend reading the Bible, going to church, or attending youth group meetings and activities. This tithe is set aside for doing work for God's kingdom. Specifically, that means helping others.

During His ministry on Earth, Jesus made it quite clear to His disciples that serving others wasn't just something they should do for good measure; it was an absolute priority. Throughout the Gospels, we see Jesus demonstrating service to others. He healed the sick, fed the multitudes, cast out demons, and touched broken hearts. He met the needs of those with whom He came into contact. He commanded the Church to do the same. And in the book of Acts, we see that the early Church made it a priority to do the same.

Some would go so far as to say that if a local congregation isn't serving the needy in their community, meeting their spiritual, physical, social, and financial needs, that local congregation isn't fulfilling the call of the Church. Granted, the church's ultimate command is to make disciples of all nations. However, it's also called to serve.

What about you? How much time have you spent serving your community? How much time have you invested in serving the hungry, teaching the illiterate, visiting prisoners, or helping the poor? If your answer is "Not much," then you're missing it.

Remember God's definition of a success? It includes putting others first. If you want to be successful in God's eyes, no matter how good your excuses might be, you've got to start serving others. Tithing your time to God is a good way to begin.

WHAT JESUS SAID ABOUT SERVING

- If anyone wants to be first, he must be the very last, and the servant of all.

  —Mark 9:35

- Whoever wants to become great among you must be your servant, and whoever wants to be first must be slave of all. For even the Son of Man did not come to be served, but to serve, and to give his life as a ransom for many.

  —Mark 10:43-45

- The greatest among you should be like the youngest, and the one who rules like the one who serves. For who is greater, the one who is at the table or the one who serves? Is it not the one who is at the table? But I am among you as one who serves.

  —Luke 22:26-27

- Blessed are the merciful, for they will be shown mercy.

  —Matthew 5:7

overcoming green-eyed greed ▮ ▮ ▮▮ ▮▮ ▮ ▮

Let's review. Success in God's eyes has nothing to do with how much you achieve. Success in God's eyes comes from total submission to His purpose and plan for your life. If a guy wants to be great in God's eyes, he must be willing to lose everything for the cause of Christ.

Want to kill any chance of being a godly success? Let greed enter your life. That's right: greed.

Greed is the overwhelming desire for money, power, and possessions. Greed is always self-centered and can never be satisfied. It always wants more and does not care how it gets it. Greed will destroy your life.

GOD'S WILL IS . . .   GREED WILL . . .

- self-sacrifice
- to always put others first
- to give to the work of His kingdom
- for you to help the needy

- lead to self-gratification
- always use others for personal gain
- cause you to keep everything for your own good
- lead you to help yourself

In Mark 10, Jesus was approached by a rich young man. This man asked Jesus what he had to do to have eternal life. Jesus told him to obey God's commandments. The young man replied that he already did all these things. Jesus' next statement couldn't have been more devastating to him. "One thing you lack," Jesus said. "Go, sell everything you have and give to the poor, and you will have treasure in heaven. Then come, follow me" (verse 21). The price was too high for the young man. He wanted his earthly possessions more than he wanted eternal life with God.

Jesus wasn't necessarily asking the man to become a pauper. He was asking him to give up his greedy lifestyle. The young man was rich and self-centered. He'd achieved great wealth in his short lifetime. But inside, he was empty. He wanted God but wasn't willing to give up his earthly possessions to have God. He loved possessions more than anything. He was greedy.

After the young man left, Jesus looked at His disciples and said, "It is easier for a camel to go through the eye of a needle than for a rich man to enter the kingdom of God" (verse 25). In other words, Jesus was saying that it's impossible for a man possessed by greed to make it into heaven! It's pretty simple in God's eyes. When a guy's greedy, he doesn't give a rip about what God wants, and as a result, he has no part in God's kingdom.

So, what about you? Ever find yourself wanting money, power, and possessions? If so, you might not be greedy yet, but you could be well on the way. Stop right now and ask God for forgiveness. Ask Him to change your heart by removing any nuggets of greed and replacing them with seeds of humility and self-sacrifice. If you really mean it, God can and will turn your life around. And anytime you catch yourself thinking like that, do it all over again. You might not change overnight, but with time, God can purify your thoughts and desires.

chapter twenty-one: HOW TO EARN MONEY | | |

Imagine strutting around in those incredible Nikes YOU earned from YOUR summer job! It would feel great to make your own money (and to pay for your own things for a change), wouldn't it? This doesn't have to be a dream. It CAN happen! But it all starts with a little planning right NOW.

We caught up with a few teens from around the country who are putting their free time to work. While these guys aren't yet millionaires, they have learned three essential "STASH-CASH SECRETS"—and were willing to share them with YOU.

StaSH-CaSH Secret no. 1: Be creative | | | | | | | |

Instead of putting your mind in neutral for the summer, get it cranked up by thinking of ways to earn a little money.

Do you like animals? Start a dog-walking business. Are you good with people? Be a greeter at a movie theater. Are you a neat freak? Follow Nate, a 17-year-old from Seattle.

from garbage boy to mr. trash

Nate lends a touch of class to his work. He's dressed in a black tux, and young fans clamor for his autograph at the Everett, Washington, Aquasox ballpark. But who is this guy?

He's Mr. Trash. With plastic garbage bag in hand, he makes it hip for fans to stow their throwaways rather than make a mess of the stadium.

"It's the perfect job!" Nate says. "I get to spend my summer working around the thing I love." (During the

school year, he feeds his craving to be on the field by playing second base for the Everett High Seagulls.) It's also the perfect solution to a costly cleanup bill for the Aquasox, the triple-A affiliate of the Seattle Mariners.

"It's a creative way to keep the place clean," says the trashmeister himself. "Why not make it fun for the fans so they'll take pride in the park?"

Stash-Cash Secret No. 2: Maximize Every Opportunity

Here's a hard fact: You're not going to enter the business world as the CEO of IBM. No, the truth is that you're probably going to start in an entry-level position. But don't get discouraged. Get that first job and work your way up. That's the plan of Jonathan, a 17-year-old native of Colorado Springs.

Happy Meals, Happy Faces!

Jonathan took a position at McDonald's because he needed a job and the restaurant was across the street from his house. But he didn't flip burgers, make fries, and take money for long.

About one month into the job, his managers pulled him aside and said, "You're good with people, and you've got a bubbly personality. Let's see what you can do with the birthday parties."

For the past year and a half, Jonathan has been golden as the birthday coordinator. "The first time I did it," Jonathan remembers, "it was incredible how much fun I had putting smiles on the kids' faces. The happier I was, the happier they became."

Jonathan has always been outgoing. Because his dad's in the military, he has lived in Texas, Germany, four places in California, Canada, and Colorado. His personality helps him make friends quickly. Although he introduces himself as Jonathan, his guests seem to prefer calling him Mr. McDonald, Ronald McDonald, or Catsup-Head—and he can joke right back with them.

"With the help of my parents—because they raised me in a God-fearing house with good morals and a level of respect—I've decided to show everybody that teens can make a difference."

BoSS

stash-cash secret no. 3: get off your can't

The biggest thing holding you back from using your talent and scoring some summertime bucks is YOU. Or to be more specific, your wrong assumption that nobody will take you seriously.

In the words of 16-year-old Trevor of Trevilians, Virginia, "Get off your CAN'T and get going."

toon boy tales

For some guys, summer in a small town like Trevilians spells B-O-R-E-D-O-M. But for Trevor, it means a lucrative opportunity.

"Summer break gives me more time to work on my cartoons," Trevor says, "which has become a business for me. And since I'm surrounded by farmers, possums, and cows, that's exactly what I draw. Especially cows."

The teen's cartoon career kicked off three years ago. At age 12, he put together a collection of his farmland funnies—along with other crazy characters, such as *Stupid Fish Gangsters*—then set out with a lofty goal: "I'm going to publish a book."

He was inspired by his favorite artists, Gary Larson *(The Far Side)* and Bill Waterston *(Calvin and Hobbes),* and was convinced that he, too, had the skill to be a published cartoonist. *Why wait until I'm 40?* he told himself. *I can do it NOW!*

His parents agreed and helped him get published with Poindexter Press, a nearby book publisher.

Today, Trevor not only has his first book to his credit, titled *Scraps,* but he also makes money selling to Virginia newspapers a toonstrip called *Cuddy*—a continuing tale about a cow. (What else?!)

"If I didn't have the courage to believe in my abilities or the persistence to pursue my dreams, I wouldn't be a published artist," Trevor says. "My advice: Don't sell yourself short. You can accomplish anything you put your mind to."

Hold the fries, guys. Here's how you can be your own boss.

1. **Start a dog-washing business.** Most families dread washing Fido. Tell friends, neighbors, and relatives that you'll gladly take this burden off their hands! WARNING: Never bathe a pooch that eyes you with a hungry, foaming-at-the-mouth smirk. ($10 per dog.)

2. **Wash cars, boats, RVs, etc.** Dirty windshields, mud-splattered paint jobs, grimy tires—no matter where you look, you're bound to find a car or camper that needs a good wash. Grab a hose, a bottle of nongritty liquid soap, and a friend. (Cars, $5; trucks, $7; campers, $10; motor homes, $15 and up.)

3. **Raise worms.** Imagine a zillion itty-bitty creatures crawling around in a dirt-filled wooden crate. No kidding—worms are easy to raise. Fill a box with dirt, manure, peat moss, and vegetable scraps. Catch a few worms from your backyard and plop them in. They'll multiply like crazy. Now sell them to fishermen, sporting goods stores, and gardeners who want to improve their soil. Just think of all the girls you can gross out! (You can get 50 to 75 cents per dozen wholesale, $1.50—plus retail.)

4. **Be a "monocotyledonous maintenance engineer" (mow lawns).** Your dad probably earned a few bucks this way too. (Depending on the lawn size, charge between $5 and $25.)

5. **Start a baby-sitting service for kids or pets.** Watching little kids isn't just a girl's job. It can be a great way for guys like you to build up your bank account. (Charge $3 to $5 per hour per kid.)

   Or say your neighbors are taking a month-long cruise across the Pacific (or a weekend at the North Pole) but can't take along Peaches, their precious parakeet. Offer to care for Peaches while they're away. Hand out a flyer in the neighborhood two weeks before summer vacation. (Negotiate the price based on length of time and how much work is involved.)

6. **Be a graphic designer for your church, club, etc.** Don't be a starving artist!

7. **Begin a grocery delivery service.** Know some senior citizens who need help getting their Wheaties? Offer your muscles for money. Busy housewives and handicapped people could also benefit from this service. (Charge $3 to $4 per hour.)

8. **Paint house numbers on curbs or flags on mailboxes.** Go to a hardware store and pick up various stencils, spray paint (boring white is the neighborhood norm), red paint, and a brush. Once you've perfected your technique and checked with city officials to see if you need a license, hit the streets! Surely nobody wants to be the only one in the neighborhood with a dingy, rusty flag or faded house numbers! (Charge $5 per house and $2 per flag.)

9. **Be a paper boy.** What other job offers travel, fresh air, and a chance to exercise your pitching arm? Try being a substitute on someone's route first to make sure you can handle the hours and responsibility.

10. **Recycle.** You may not get rich doing this, but it's an easy way to pick up a few extra bucks. People love to get rid of the cans, bottles, and newspapers collecting in their garage. All you have to do is ask. Plus, keep your eyes peeled for stuff on the street or garbage in park trash cans that can be recycled. Start collecting!

chapter twenty-two: DOLLARS AND SENSE ▌▌▌ ▌

Get this: During the year 2000, teenagers in the United States alone spent more than $155 billion. (That's according to Teenage Research Unlimited.) YIKES!

On average, most teens spent about $84 per week. More than two-thirds of that they had earned on their own. Only about a third, or $27 of that $84, was their parents' money.

Some financial analysts believe that the $155 billion figure could increase by 20 or 30 percent over the next five years. That's a lot of cash floating around—all controlled by teenagers.

Because youth represent a huge portion of their market, retailers pay advertisers lots of money to convince you to buy their products. It's the advertisers' job to make you think you need a certain product more than you need to save your money. That's right. They don't want you to keep your money. They want it—all of it. And they'll stop at nothing to make you think you should throw your hard-earned cash in their direction. The scary thing is, historically, they're pretty good at what they do. Like thousands of other teens, you've seen a commercial or an advertisement in a magazine and thought, I just gotta have that! Then, right after you thought that, you've probably gone out and purchased the thing in the ad. See what we mean?

But after you buy something that you've "just gotta have," how long do you use it? Did you purchase it on a whim? (You know, sort of an impulse thing?) Think that's no big deal? Remember that $84-a-week figure most teens are supposed to have to spend? Rather than blowing it all on stuff you won't be using in a month, if you saved just half of it—$42 a week—at the end of one year you would have $2,184. That's not including interest if it was put in a simple savings account.

So, if you started doing this at age 12, then by the time you turned 16, you'd have nearly $9,000! And if you place your money in a savings account or a certificate of deposit that pays only 4 percent in interest, you can add another $600 to $700! Assuming you were really thrifty and were able to occasionally put away more than $42 a week, you can safely estimate that in four years you could have over $10,000!

STEWARDSHIP—WHAT IS IT? ▌ ▌▌▌ ▌▌ ▌ ▌

A steward is one who manages another's property, finances, or affairs. So stewardship refers to how a person handles himself in a particular job.

From a biblical perspective, if Christians believe that God is the owner of all that exists and that He provides them with all their needs, then they are stewards of what He gives them. Stewardship is how Christians handle those resources.

If we look at the way Jesus taught and the things He said, good stewardship is the theme that comes through overwhelmingly. Jesus often taught by telling parables or stories to illustrate an important point. Of the almost 40 parables Jesus told, about half of them use money, resources, time, and ability to demonstrate spiritual truths.

THE PRODIGAL SPENDTHRIFT

In Luke 15:11-32, Jesus shares one of His most famous parables, the one about the prodigal son. In case you're unfamiliar with it, here's a brief recap:

There was once man a who had two sons. The younger son came to him and said, "Dad, I don't want to wait until you're dead to get my inheritance. I'd like it now, if you don't mind." So the dad gave the younger son his half of the family inheritance.

The younger son then left home for a faraway country, taking his inheritance and everything else he owned with him. When he got to where he was going, he went wild. He blew every bit of money he had in self-gratifying parties and unrestrained living. He didn't invest one dime and wound up completely broke.

Then the country he was living in went into a severe famine. With no money and no one to turn to, the only way he could survive was to take a job with a local farmer feeding the pigs. Even that didn't pay him enough to put food in his stomach. In fact, the pigs ate better than he did. Eventually, he came to his senses and realized that the servants in his own father's house lived 10 times better than he was currently living. He decided to go home and beg his father to employ him as one of the servants.

When he stepped foot on the long driveway to his house, his father saw him coming and was so excited that he ran out to meet him, kissing him and hugging him. The son was repentant and about to ask if he could simply be made a worker when the father shouted orders to the nearby servants. "Get my finest suit of clothing, clean this boy up, and put my best on him. Then go, make preparations for a major banquet because my son, who I thought was dead, has come back. Tonight we're going to celebrate his return!"

This particular parable is often used to illustrate the incredible mercy and grace God extends to humanity. And though that is the main point, within the course of the story Jesus buries a great lesson on how God views self-indulgent spending.

If you miss everything else with this parable, don't miss this. The father in this story (who represents God) is the one who owned all the wealth. The younger son takes the father's hard-earned wealth and squanders it. He blows every last penny on himself. He doesn't invest anything! And when he's completely bankrupt, when he realizes what a horrible steward he has been with his father's money, then he understands just how badly he has behaved.

The critical issue here is that God expects us to be good stewards with what He gives us. When we live like there's no tomorrow, spending all our money and time on useless items and ventures, then we're living far outside of God's will for our lives. As in the parable of the prodigal son, even though we can find forgiveness for that kind of lifestyle, God will not bless us as long as we continue to live like that.

Does that mean a guy can't spend anything on himself? No. God doesn't have a problem with you indulging yourself on occasion. But it does mean that God expects you to use wisely the assets He grants you. He wants you to invest first into His kingdom, tithing and giving to the work of the Church. Then God wants you to put some of your assets away for safekeeping, for those times when money might get tight. He also wants you to support your family and pay all your bills on time, when they're due (that's something most teens guys don't have to worry about right now, but it's never too early to be thinking about it). After all that, God is cool if you indulge yourself with what's left over.

SPENDING VERSUS SAVING ▌ ▌▌ ▌▌ ▌ ▌

According to a survey taken on-line by both Nickelodeon and MTV, teens are doing much better at saving their money than most people thought. For those surveyed in the 13-21 age-group, an average of 25 percent of their total income was put into savings. On the other hand, according to another survey done by the Consumer Federation, most adults receive a failing grade where savings is concerned. In fact, the U.S. personal saving rate—which is savings as a percentage of after-tax income—fell to a record *negative* 8 percent in the year 2001! So, how much are teens saving each year? Here's what the survey said:

teen saving Habits

Age Group	Amount Saved per Year	Percent of Income Saved
13-15	$260	16%
16-17	$1,196	28%
18-21	$2,600	33%

*"U.S. Online Youth Spend $164 Billion Annually, " Business Wire, May 15, 2001. (www.businesswire.com/webbox/bw.091100/202553087.htm)

making money: three goals ▮ ▮▮▮ ▮▮ ▮ ▮

What if a guy wanted to save up 10K in cool cash? How would he go about it? The first thing he'd need to do would be to *set goals*. You might be thinking, *That's easy! His goal is to save $10,000. Next question.* True, that may be the ultimate goal he is reaching for, but in this case, the goals can be broken down into these three categories:

1. The **reason** goal
2. The **time** goal
3. The **monthly** goal

the reason goal

If you wanted to save $10,000, it might help to have a reason behind it. This reason gives further motivation to save it. Remember, those advertisers out there are trying to convince you that they need your money more than you do. If you have a reason you're keeping your money, it makes it less tempting to spend it frivolously.

Before you decide what your reason is going to be, maybe you should take some time to pray about it. God really does want us to look to Him in all our decisions. He knows what He'd like for you to become in your future life. The decisions you make today will affect that future. Maybe God wants you to save to purchase a car. Or maybe He wants you to save for college or trade school. God really will direct your decision in this, and it will always be a wise one.

the time goal

Now that you know what to save for, what does it actually cost? If it costs more than $10,000, you'll need to increase your ultimate goal. If it costs less, you're free to lower that goal (or keep it the same and use the excess for some other goal). As stated earlier in this chapter, if a guy put about $42 a week (roughly $182 a month) into savings, he could probably store up $10,000 in about four years.

Patience is key. Storing up $10,000 doesn't happen overnight. Having a specific time frame in which you need to obtain your ultimate goal will help your spending habits. In other words, if you're 12 years old and are saving 10 grand to help with your college expenses, you have more than four years to do that. On the other hand, if you're 16 and saving for college, you're going to have to more than double your $42-a-week effort! You have only about two years to knock it out.

the monthly goal

Now figure out what your monthly goal will be to put in savings. The setting of this goal begins by taking a realistic look at your monthly financial picture. How much money do you bring in each month? Do you get an allowance? Do you have a job? Do you get money for doing extra chores around the house? Add all this up. That's your monthly income.

Next, figure out your monthly expenses. Set aside your tithe and offerings. Remember, God wants us to be good stewards with what He gives to us. That means, first and foremost, giving back to the work of God's kingdom. Then total up your other monthly expenditures. If you have a car, do you have to pay for the gas or insurance? If you don't drive, your expenditures might be your lunches at school or class and laboratory fees. Do you go to the movies occasionally? The arcade? Buy video games or hang out at McDonald's with your friends? Total all those projected costs for the month.

When you've done that, subtract those expenses from your monthly income. What's left over is what you have to put in savings each month. If you don't have enough left over to reach your ultimate goal within the time frame you've determined, you'll have to adjust your spending habits or figure out a way to bring in some extra money.

FIVE EASY WAYS TO SAVE EXTRA CASH

1. At the end of the day, empty your pocket change into your old, reliable piggy bank. Don't ever raid your piggy bank unless your intent is to put that cash into a real bank to begin drawing interest.

2. When your grandparents or family friends give you extra cash for your birthday or Christmas, instead of spending it, put it in the bank and don't touch it.

3. It might sound silly, but use those coupons that come in the newspaper or the mail when you're going out to eat with your friends at the local fast food joint. Put the difference of what you'd normally spend in your savings account. Hey, it's your money. Don't spend more of it than you have to.

4. When your parents give you money to purchase a new pair of jeans (or whatever), ask them if you can put the difference in savings if you can find a bargain. If they agree, go to the discount stores and locate the best deal you can find. Make sure you ask before you try this tactic, though. It's your parents' money you're dealing with in this case, not yours.

5. Take all those trinkets, toys, and clothes you don't use anymore to a consignment shop and sell them. Or have a garage sale. You'd be surprised how well you can do with this.

HOW TO SPEND WISELY

Bottom line: You can save money only if you don't spend it. When you hear that a store is having a sale and that you can save lots of money if you "BUY NOW AND DON'T DELAY," keep in mind that you're probably being fed a lie—a lie that will end up lining the pockets of someone else.

To keep from spending more than you have to, try doing the following:

- **Never buy anything on impulse.** If it seems like a deal you just can't pass up, usually it's a deal you should pass up.

- **Always ask yourself a few questions before you make a purchase.** Ask stuff like *Do I really need this?* and *Can I get by without spending this money?*

- **Never carry large amounts of cash with you when you're going out—unless it's an absolute must that you do so.** It's less tempting to spend if you don't have it.

- **When you step into a store, make your purchase and get out as quickly as possible.** Don't give yourself a chance to be tempted to spend more than you should. (The same goes for stores on the Web.)

- **Don't buy what you can get for free.** In other words, don't purchase music CDs, video games, DVDs, or videos if you can borrow them from a friend or library or rent them for much cheaper. What's hot today will be lame tomorrow. Don't waste money on it.

Go At Focus on the Family, we are committed to helping you learn more about Jesus Christ and preparing you to change your world for Him! We realize the struggles you face are different from your parent's, or your little brother's, so Focus on the Family has developed a ton of stuff specifically for you! They'll get you ready to boldly live out your faith no matter what situation you find yourself in.

We don't want to tell you what to do. We want to encourage and equip you to be all God has called you to be in every aspect of life! That may involve strengthening your relationship with God, solidifying your values and perhaps making some serious changes in your heart and mind.

We'd like to come alongside you as you consider God's role in your life, discover His plan for you in the lives of others and how you can impact your generation to change the world.

We have Web sites, magazines, palm-sized topical booklets, fiction books, a live call-in radio show ... all dealing with the topics and issues that you deal with and care about. For a more detailed listing of what we have available to you, visit our Web site at **www.family.org.** Then click on 'resources,' followed by either 'teen girls' or 'teen guys.'